THE
EQUIPPING
CHURCH

Also Available

The Equipping Church Guidebook

THE EQUIPPING CHURCH

SERVING TOGETHER TO TRANSFORM LIVES

Sue
Mallory

GRAND RAPIDS, MICHIGAN 49530

ZONDERVAN™

The Equipping Church
Copyright © 2001 by Leadership Network, Inc.

Requests for information should be addressed to:

Zondervan, *Grand Rapids, Michigan 49530*

Library of Congress Cataloging-in-Publication Data

Mallory, Sue.
    The equipping church : serving together to transform lives / Sue Mallory.
      p. cm.
    Includes bibliographical references.
    ISBN 0-310-24067-0 (hardcover)
    1. Lay ministry. I. Title.
  BV677 .M35 2001
  253—dc 21   2001026584

This edition is printed on acid-free paper.

Interior design by Nancy Wilson

Printed in the United States of America

---

01 02 03 04 05 06 /❖ DC/ 10 9 8 7 6 5 4 3 2 1

To Charles Shields—
mentor, teacher, challenger, and friend

Contents

Foreword

THE POINT OF CHURCH GROWTH is not to collect new people and cage them with church programs. The goal of church health is not to fatten up church members for show. *That was then. This is now.* The church exists to equip people in order to release them back into the world, grounded in truth and community, dangerous for the gospel. God has created a new movement of churches that equip people, according to their calling and gifts, to be salt and light in their churches, communities, family, workplace, media, and government—in the whole of society.

Bob Buford founded Leadership Network (LN) in response to the question, "How can I be useful to God's kingdom?" Over the last seventeen years, LN has developed a reputation for identifying and connecting the innovative leaders of today's church. Leadership Training Network (LTN), a partner organization with Leadership Network, was formed six years ago with a commitment to equipping church leaders to empower and mobilize God's people into biblical, gift-based team service.

In *The Equipping Church*, Sue Mallory, a founding member of LTN, tells the story of the development of this movement of God—a movement marked by shared ministry between pastor and people . . . a movement marked by a biblical conviction to be the church, faithful and focused . . . a movement marked by a commitment to community, caring, and compassion. Sue communicates God's work through the lens of her story of developing an equipping ministry as a part of the team at Brentwood Presbyterian Church in Los Angeles, California.

You are going to love this book because you will feel the heartbeat of God as Sue articulates the challenges and victories, the joy and struggles, that mark the journey toward building an equipping church *where people serve together to transform lives.* You are going to love this book because you will walk away with life-changing principles you can apply immediately in your church. I know, because not only have I read the book, I've heard the stories from Sue directly. And I know because much of what happens at Windsor Village UMC in Houston is a result of the application of the equipping church principles articulated in these pages.

If you desire to be a part of the movement of God that includes churches not only talking about but also demonstrating a track record of discipleship on the streets, churches that measure their success not on numbers of attendees or persons committed to various church programs but rather on how their efforts make a difference in reducing the crime rate of their community, churches that are committed to bridging the economic divide of their city and communicating that the compassion of Christ is real in meeting immediate and eternal needs, then read on.

Kirbyjon Caldwell, senior pastor,
Windsor Village United Methodist Church,
Houston, Texas

Acknowledgments

THROUGHOUT MY LIFE I've been blessed with many mentors and role models who have brought me to the place of writing this book. Who I have become is a direct result of their wisdom, love, modeling, and belief in me. I thank God for each one's imprint on my life.

The women in my life—my grandmother, my mother, and my two sisters—modeled commitment and unconditional love and support. But perhaps the most important thing I learned from them was that success was about an inner strength and a deep belief bigger than adverse circumstances or academic credentials.

My husband, Bob, has been the greatest mentor, teacher, and friend I could have ever hoped for. Your belief in me and in what I could accomplish has always been far greater than my own and has become the benchmark toward which I strive. Your sacrifice in my becoming who God created me to be has been nothing short of monumental. There are no words to adequately convey my gratitude and my love.

My children by birth, marriage, and God's grace have been my greatest cheerleaders, affirming and valuing my "second calling" into full-time ministry as strongly as they did my first calling—full-time motherhood. I love you all.

The people of Brentwood Presbyterian Church—my covenant family—invited me into ministry. I owe such special gratitude to all of you, staff (past and present) and congregation alike, for allowing me to serve, make mistakes, flounder, and ultimately flourish in your midst. This book is your story.

To Bob Buford, founder of Leadership Network, thank you for your heart for the church, your commitment to make her healthier, and your willingness to risk the creation of Leadership Training Network.

Brad Smith has mentored me into the beauty of the expanded world of faith across all denominational divides. Through your modeling I learned the power of character and the power of prayer in reconciliation, bridge building, and relationship building. Thanks, Brad, for your grace, your humility, and your limitless patience and humor—and for teaching me "the formula."

Thanks to the awesome LTN team: the staff—Sarah Bicknell, Carolyn Cochran, Greg Ligon—and the faculty—Sally Vasen Alter, Leroy Armstrong, Preston Bright, Kim Clegg, Chris Hardy, Barbara Harris,

Tammy Kelley, Don Simmons, Ian Stevenson, and Calvie Hughson Schwalm—who have been the authentic practitioners/leaders who have breathed life into God's equipping movement. Thank you for your passion for equipping God's people, your love, and your outrageous laughter. You are the greatest team I've ever had the privilege to be a part of.

To Neil Wilson, whose gentle spirit, pastor's heart, and extraordinary gift of listening helped make this book a reality, my profound and heartfelt thanks.

To my spiritual mentor and soul mate, Jackie McNabb, thank you for your love, for your unwavering faith in me, for always taking me back to the Scriptures, and for constantly reminding me of God's call on my life.

And to a very special band of encouragers (my husband fondly refers to them as "the boys")—Bruce Bugbee, Paul Ford, Alan Nelson, and Greg Ogden—thank you all for extending your hearts to welcome me as a partner in ministry. I treasure your friendship, your encouragement, and your prayers.

Finally, to Nadia, Sarah, Elizabeth, Pauline, and Carroll Shields for sharing the most important person in your lives with so many that we might more fully understand God's radical grace and be challenged to become more like him.

Introduction

WHEN I SET OUT to write a book about lay ministry, I wanted to avoid using the word *lay*. Laity may be a term with a noble past, but it has a present identity crisis. It tends to appear in sentences where phrases such as "not very good," "not professional," "common," and "second-class" might easily be used in its place. In fact, I put off writing this book for a long time because I wasn't sure I had an audience or the right to speak. After all, I thought, I'm just a layperson. Just a layperson?—I had to learn to think again.

God has graciously filled my life with people who corrected my misunderstanding. If I use the word *just* in my self-description as a way of indicating that I might not have anything of value to say, I have invited others to reach that same conclusion before they have even heard what I have to say. There are certain phrases in which *just* simply doesn't fit. How could I diminish my Creator by saying, "I'm just a child of God"? How could I diminish my Savior by saying, "I'm just someone for whom Christ died"? I won't. And I won't diminish the amazing fellowship into which I have been called by saying I'm just a layperson. Wonder of wonders, I'm actually a layperson. I'm actually one of many called into the body of Christ to be a member. I get to serve and to be served. I share the same entry point and status with every other believer. My duties and gifts may be unique, but I share with all other believers the priceless gift of belonging to Christ. So when I use the word *lay* in this book, I want those who read it to understand that I have come to see it as a title of honor.

Before writing this book on lay ministry, though, I also discovered I had a problem with the word *ministry*. In my quest for a new term for "laypeople," I overlooked another tendency shared by most of the body of Christ. We hesitate calling what we do for Christ *ministry*. My pastor shattered that tendency in me by consistently treating the people in our congregation as real ministers. An unforgettable learning moment for me came when I got to know a new person in our church I'll call Joe.

Joe began attending our church shortly after he was diagnosed on the downhill slide toward death from AIDS. In our crowded sanctuary he might have gone unnoticed, except that we have some gifted people among us who notice. They approach and welcome strangers in ways that feel natural and real. They joyfully exercise the gift of hospitality. They are masters of a priceless art. Under their attention, Joe didn't stay a stranger long. He found a spiritual home.

Partly because of my own medical history and partly because I was involved in the training of those who were embracing many different kinds of outreach in our church, I became part of Joe's life. One of the important lessons that Joe confirmed was the truth that people usually enter our churches with deep needs. They are hurting, seeking, hiding, wounded. A visitor rarely turns out to be a fresh reinforcement sent to immediately fill a vital spot on the front lines in our church. A visitor more often is a casualty of other battles in other places, hoping to discover hope and find healing when he or she walks through our doors.

Joe was wounded and dying. We didn't know his whole story at the time, but we were learning to meet needs before expecting participation. Joe signed up for a membership class. He was enthusiastic. But he didn't show up. That's when the advancing stages of his illness became known to some of us.

Because we had purposely decided that people who needed long-term care were not to be among the direct duties of the senior pastoral staff in our church, I accepted the task of keeping track of Joe's needs and making sure we met them as well as possible. I sought training in dealing with AIDS patients. I discovered that they need the same care as patients who are dying of other illnesses. Joe and I became friends. I reported to the church that his desire to join us in membership was both real and impossible with our present structure. He wasn't well enough to attend the classes. I asked the leadership to make an exception, assuring them that I would take the class material to Joe and prepare him for the membership vows. I told them that Joe didn't have much time, but that he wanted to die as part of our church family. They responded with compassionate support.

Joe and I had a wonderful time of spiritual sharing and mutual growth in the following weeks. He became a member of our church. His spiritual life blossomed even as his physical health deteriorated. Our relationship grew. The flow of goodness went both ways. Joe was giving as well as receiving. During this same time, my mother was seriously ill, and the stress of those days was somehow relieved by the hours spent in conversation with Joe. He knew about pain. He knew loss. He knew me.

During one particularly stressful day, when my mother's life seemed to be hanging by a thread, I got an urgent message that Joe was dying. I immediately called the church to alert one of the pastors. They were not available. I left messages for them at every number and on every answering machine I could reach. I hurried to Joe's home.

When I arrived, I met several of Joe's friends. They had gathered to keep him company in his last hours. Joe's room was a place of hopeful sadness. Light and flowers added brightness. Wonderful music filled the space. I prayed with him, and we sat quietly for a couple of hours. At one point I was called to the phone, hopeful that it was one of the pastors. Instead, Joe's sister was calling from a distant airport, on her way, concerned that Joe not be alone. I assured her that he was with friends and that his church family was supporting him in prayer. During all of this I was keenly aware that my time was limited and that the pastors were not showing up. Each telephone ring in the other room brought a moment of hope, but no clergy materialized. I stayed as long as I could. When the time came for me to leave, I prayed with Joe again. I realized he was at peace and that he wouldn't be alone. I returned to my mother's bedside.

I found out later that Joe died about fifteen minutes after I had left. His departure was peaceful. I was upset. Why hadn't any of our pastors made it to his bedside? When I had a free moment later in the evening, I called our senior pastor, Charles, at home. He waited patiently throughout my holy tirade. After allowing me to vent my frustration over his absence from Joe's bedside, Charles gave me time to take a breath and then said quietly, "Sue, I called Joe's house when I received your message. The person who answered assured me that the minister was already with Joe. That was you, Sue. Why should I go when God had already provided someone to minister to Joe?"

I was stunned. Charles caught me doing ministry, and he had the wisdom to point it out. He trusted me in a situation where he could have easily moved in and taken over. Instead, he had the joy of knowing that a person he had helped equip for ministry was actually doing it!

The people in your church need to have that kind of overwhelming sense of shock. They need to experience the joy of having someone call what they do for Christ *ministry*. They need to be taught and then caught serving the Lord. They need that significance and worth. Why? Because ministry is their birthright as believers. The freedom we all have in Christ affects not only our position with God; it deeply affects our place in the world. We become Christ's representatives. The way in which our obedience to Christ affects the world deserves to be called ministry.

According to Ephesians 4:11–13 there is some doubt about whether the main function of pastors is to do ministry at all, in the way we frequently use the term *ministry*. For ministry is service, and this key passage in Scripture directs pastors and others to prepare God's people for works of ministry. If this book on lay ministry has any positive effect at all, it will be to increase the number of believers who discover that they were called to be ministers for Christ, and it will motivate their pastors to have a new passion to prepare them for that work!

EQUIPPING PRINCIPLES

AT THE END OF EACH chapter I'll summarize some of the key equipping principles I've illustrated through my story and the stories of others. Your experiences and results will not be identical to anyone else's. But the underlying biblical and practical principles will be present anytime equipping ministry becomes a reality.

EQUIPPING HEROES

THROUGH LEADERSHIP TRAINING NETWORK I've had the opportunity and privilege to visit, learn from, and train many different churches and denominations across the United States and Canada.

Throughout the book and at the end of each chapter are examples from a wide cross section of these churches that differ in size, denomination, and church culture. Each illustrates and models the principles of a biblically functioning equipping church. As you will discover, there is not one "right way," but rather many variations of the same principles— just as there is not one gift, but many unique wonderful gifts, all essential to the body (see Romans 12:4–8).

- Pleasant Hills Community Presbyterian Church, Pittsburgh, Pennsylvania
- Grace Community Church, Noblesville, Indiana
- First United Methodist Church, Bixby, Oklahoma
- Lake Pointe Baptist Church, Rockwall, Texas
- Willow Creek Community Church, Barrington, Illinois
- Calvary Church, St. Louis, Missouri
- Oak Hills Church of Christ, San Antonio, Texas
- St. Monica's Catholic Church, Santa Monica, California
- First Presbyterian Church of Bellevue, Bellevue, Washington
- St. Gerard Majella Catholic Church, Port Jefferson Station, New York
- Church of the Resurrection, Leawood, Kansas
- First Baptist Church of Leesburg, Leesburg, Florida
- Heartland Community Church, Overland Park, Kansas
- Ginghamsburg United Methodist Church, Tipp City, Ohio
- Windsor Village United Methodist Church, Houston, Texas

1

Starting the Journey in Helplessness

SOME OF MY REGULAR holy moments these days occur in my car, far from my church building. My husband and I are among the privileged who drive our pastor to radiation treatments. The gradual advance of cancer has recently forced him to give up the formal title of *pastor* in our church. Charles no longer preaches. He doesn't have to—his entire life has become a sermon.

We talk a lot during these trips to the hospital. Actually, I do most of the talking; he does most of the listening. But when he does speak, I know he has been listening. I reflect on all that God is doing in the church today; Charles thinks about all that God will do to get him through today. I'm excited about the ministry to which God has called me; Charles is overwhelmed by all the ways in which God's people are ministering to him. I'm driven by the vision of the body of Christ being all that it can be; Charles is a humble participant in and beneficiary of that vision coming to reality in his corner of the world.

My pastor, Charles, and I share a lot of history in our parallel walks with God. We've come a long way in the last two decades. In a startling way, God has almost exactly reversed our roles. Many of us who have learned so much from Charles over the years now have the honor of ministering to him. He taught us a lot about ministry; now we get to practice on him.

BEFORE THE VISION

I BEGAN THIS JOURNEY into ministry in what I have come to see as the perfect starting place: helplessness. My own faith development occurred

17

in a three-generation home. We lived with my grandparents after my parents' marriage broke up. I was deeply affected by the unshakable faith of my grandparents, as well as by the ambivalence of my mother, whose divorce had been handled by her church in a demeaning way. Her pain was deep. I wasn't always able to sort out my yearnings to trust the Lord of the church from my fears and other feelings connected to the people of the church. I gradually became the kind of person who belonged to the church but wasn't exactly sure how the church belonged to me.

My first awareness of helplessness came to me when as a young mother I felt the weight of responsibility for my children's faith. It grew as I wondered about bringing my kids up in the neighborhood church we had attended for several years. There seemed so little there that I could enthusiastically pass on to my children. It never occurred to me that the church might change or that I might have a role in that change. All I knew was that some kind of change needed to happen. I wanted my children exposed to a faith that would challenge and sustain them.

God graciously answered a prayer for which I had no words. A friend invited us to visit her church, which was some distance from our home, because she knew I was concerned about the needs of our family. She was excited about the signs of life that were appearing in her congregation. My family and I arrived at the church we now call home looking for some kind of visible spiritual vitality. We almost immediately sensed an intangible difference. We saw people taking God seriously— and having fun at the same time. A glimmer of hope was beginning to intrude on my first stage of helplessness.

I didn't realize it at the time, but Brentwood Presbyterian Church was just hitting stride again after two years without a pastor. The new minister was in place, and the impact of his ministry style was beginning to be felt. Our first impressions probably revealed more about our needs than about the church. We were captivated by the new, the different—the life we observed and the welcome we received.

We found a young pastor preaching passionately about what he called "the priesthood of believers." I thought he had invented a new and exciting concept. Soon he showed me in 1 Peter 2:4–5 that he was actually preaching an ancient biblical principle.

Charles wasn't preaching a plan or a program but holding a truth before us like a diamond. He was leading us around the gem called "the priesthood of believers" and inviting us to view it from every angle. I sensed somehow that this truth about God's plan for believers might hold the answer for what I was longing to experience in the Christian journey. I thought I was ready for the next step. It turned out to be a huge step backward. God used a painful and unexpected detour to take me where he wanted me to go.

Before I could mentally deal with the significance of what I was hearing in church, I was ambushed by an overwhelming health challenge. A seemingly minor accident led to long-term, life-changing complications. Over a two-year period of debilitating pain I experienced deterioration of my jaws and severe accompanying headaches. Helplessness returned with a vengeance. A bewildering maze of diagnoses led to the first of several reconstructive surgeries for ruptured and fused disks in my jaws, which left me temporarily disabled. You could literally say that I was laid off from my multifaceted job as the mother of young children. Necessities like cooking, cleaning, and mothering became impossibilities. For a time life was divided into three phases: times when I couldn't speak because I needed surgery, times when I couldn't speak because I had just had surgery, and brief times when I could speak and tried to get everything said as quickly as possible before the cycle repeated itself. My self-understanding as a competent person took a severe blow. Pain-free living faded into a memory. I was faced with a shattering inability to meet my family's needs.

Almost before I could wonder where to turn, people from church showed up, took over, and did what I couldn't do. They served cheerfully and practically. They changed our lives. Just like that; no fanfare or warning. They met our needs faster than I can tell the story and more completely than words can describe. On some of my lowest days, when helplessness and frustration presented unanswerable questions, God showed me that he could settle a complex argument with a casserole, that he could defeat doubt by means of a quiet friend who sits in silence, offering merely the gift of presence.

I had never experienced the church in action like this. We had never been loved in such ways by people who barely knew us. I still marvel to think that my children have grown up knowing that people in the body of Christ really care for each other. They know the community of Christ as so much more than a theological idea. For them, it's life! For me, helplessness became the hard teacher I learned to appreciate because it taught me that Christian service is not one among many options, but it is central to God's call in our lives. The possibility that I too might experience the joy of serving became a driving force to get me healthy again.

I look back on those days of pain and inactivity with a sense of awe. God imparted an emphatic lesson to me through the messages of my pastors, the misery of my condition, and the ministry of fellow believers: The body of Christ lives by mutual giving and receiving. And I had a lot to learn about receiving as well as about giving.

I came out of that unanticipated detour and rehab time with a commitment to make sure others experienced the joy of being served as I had been served. I, who had been given so much, longed to find a place where I in turn could give. I didn't know what this "giving" would look like, but I knew it could happen because it had happened to me.

My lessons were far from over, as helplessness became a familiar companion during recurring deterioration of my jaw, ineffective solutions, and further surgeries that punctuated the next twenty years. I came to understand the simple paradox that one of the preliminary requirements for equipping ministry is a deep awareness of helplessness. Those who do not recognize their helplessness tend to resist asking for help. Those who try to do life entirely on their own find it hard to accept the very real help they need. Those who are very capable of doing a lot sometimes miss the joy of seeing how much more they can accomplish working with others. What's more, those who deny their helplessness may not even seek what they need from God.

One of the preliminary requirements for equipping ministry is a deep awareness of helplessness.

THE VISION COMES TO LIFE

DURING THAT TIME FRAME (around the year 1985), Charles had already been pastoring our church for several years. He was discerning that the people needed help to take the next step in order to apply the biblical principles about the priesthood of believers. He believed that believers would serve if given the right opportunities. He wasn't sure what the process would look like, but he knew it was how God was calling him to lead. He began looking for someone in our congregation who might be interested in discovering what a lay-driven church would look like and how it would act. The quest each of us was on led to the wonderful collision of our lives.

The history and memories Charles and I shared during our drives to the hospital began with those early days and tentative decisions. But it goes far beyond what God has done within Brentwood Presbyterian Church. The vision of equipping churches has taken shape in different places in such unique ways that we now only point to basic biblical principles and smile at all the ways God brings the living body into reality in unusual places with amazing people.

What follows begins with our initial vision and traces our journey to the present. Along the way we've discovered that God has been doing

> **The vision of equipping churches has taken shape
> in different places in such unique ways that we
> now only point to basic biblical principles and smile
> at all the ways God brings the living body into reality
> in unusual places with amazing people.**

similar things in many other churches. We share lessons in common, but specific local applications vary considerably. If you have been longing to participate or pastor in an equipping church, I want to help and encourage you in this book. But the corporate ministry God desires to bring about through you and the believers around you will be a tribute to him. It will bear God's unique stamp in your unique place. It will take your breath away!

EQUIPPING PRINCIPLES

Equipping Is Not a Program

I will tell you this more than once: Equipping ministry is not new, nor is it a program. It is a way of doing and being the church. Much of what you will read in this book was discovered by trial and error. Perhaps "rediscovered" says it better. The principles that I and countless others are still learning have been woven into the fabric of faith by the Lord of the church.

Equipping ministry is not a format that you can "plug and play." If you think that "team ministry" is the next add-on for your church, please think again. The principles you read at the end of each chapter will warn, prepare, and direct you, but they won't give you a simple program.

God has already done work where you are. The pieces that will make up dynamic equipping ministry are in your church right now. The equippers, the equipped, and the yet-to-be equipped are all around you. Some are hidden, some are misused, some are tired, and some are abused—which leads me to remind you that as a pastor, director of equipping ministries, leader of such an assortment, or church member wanting to share your gifts, your healthiest initial attitude should be one of humble helplessness. Ask God to work through you to produce a healthy example of his body. Every part of the body belongs to God; every part is there for a reason. Your joyful challenge is to help each member discover that reason!

Equipping Is Not Denominational

While I am a Presbyterian layperson, the equipping church is not particularly Presbyterian. As you will no doubt note, my story will have a Presbyterian flavor and language to it, but the last few years' experiences and study have taught me that the equipping church can take root anywhere. It can honor and transform across all denominational lines.

The equipping church represents one of those core biblical mandates that demand attention. More often than not, as I have discovered in the *Presbyterian Book of Order,* the documents of many traditions acknowledge the biblical sanction for a robust participation in ministry by the laity. The loss of lay ministry can be explained or blamed on many factors, and I will do my best to suggest some remedies along the way in this book. But the energy of the laity can best be employed today in reclaiming what was temporarily lost. The affirmation must be renewed almost daily: Lay ministry is not a denominational distinctive, but a biblical pattern and command.

Equipping Is Team Oriented

This principle functions everywhere and will get a lot of attention in the chapters that follow. You will not have a local church based on the biblical model without some kind of team mind-set. The word *equipping* immediately assumes a team model—those who do the equipping and those who are being equipped. One group needs the other. They form a team.

Once you begin to look in Scripture for the guidelines and images of what Christ had in mind for his body, you will be struck by how often the pictures are corporate, not individual. Individuals have certain significant roles in the body, but no individual is the body. When we are "in Christ," as the Bible so often expresses it, we are *in* with a whole lot of other folk! We are meant to be a team.

Equipping Is Not Quick or Easy

If you are looking for a quick fix for a struggling church, you will not find it in the equipping church model. If you are looking for the truth and for church as God designed it to be, you will find the equipping church model a biblically sound, historically tested, and workable vision for the body of Christ in action. But getting there won't be easy. That's why a shared *vision for what can be* must be part of the original plan.

EQUIPPING HEROES

Pleasant Hills Community Presbyterian Church
Pittsburgh, Pennsylvania
Vital Churches Institute: www.vitalchurches.com
Senior Pastor: E. Stanley Ott

Possessing a passion for a vital church, Stan Ott infected the people, beginning with the leadership, with a vision for what was possible in the shift from a traditional to a transformational church. His methodology was one of "bless and add," blending the best of the past and adding features that would meet the needs of the people today. Each week he modeled this in Sunday worship by blending traditional and contemporary aspects of worship.

The process began in Pleasant Hills with discovering the needs of people, employing effective principles, and establishing new practices. Through intense study of Scripture and listening to leaders in his church, Stan identified seven vital signs for a healthy church modeled by New Testament churches in Jerusalem, Ephesus, and Antioch:

1. Spirit driven
2. Biblically based
3. Discipleship directed
4. Need responsive
5. "Gathered-scattered" attentive
6. Principle patterned
7. Reflectively practiced

Through preaching, teaching, modeling, and intense prayer Pleasant Hills made the transition (though not always easily) from a pastor-centered ministry to one of shared staff and lay leadership. Small groups were essential to the process and became a part of the DNA of both Pleasant Hills and all the "vital churches" I have encountered. The growth in numbers and in the lives of people has been significant. Stan has multiplied his learning through the creation of the Vital Churches Institute, thereby helping hundreds of church leaders claim the vision for a biblically based equipping church. In a day when mainline churches are declining at a staggering rate, it is exciting to see such a powerful exception to the rule at Pleasant Hills.

QUESTIONS FOR REFLECTION AND DISCUSSION

1. Is equipping ministry a value in your church? How is it demonstrated?

2. Reflect on those whom God has grown in ministry, even through helplessness. How and where can these people now take their place among the royal priesthood?

3. Is team ministry a value in your church? What will it take to become more effective and authentic in order to see team ministry penetrate all areas of your church?

4. What evidence exists that your people understand they are a part of a royal priesthood?

2

When the Church
Is Healthy,
She Dances

He handed out gifts of apostle, prophet, evangelist, and
pastor-teacher to train Christians in skilled servant work,
working within Christ's body, the church, until we're all
moving rhythmically and easily with each other, efficient and
graceful in response to God's Son, fully mature adults, fully
developed within and without, fully alive like Christ.

Ephesians 4:11–13 THE MESSAGE

HOW CAN THIS BIBLE PASSAGE that so obviously describes the church
receive so little genuine attention? The passage may get preached often
enough, but how often does a local church actually seek to define and
shape herself according to Paul's outline? From this point on in this book
I will highlight how each chapter's theme relates to an aspect of this key
text for the equipping church.

Notice, for instance, the exciting vision of a healthy, effective
church. In Eugene Peterson's picturesque paraphrase the body of Christ
exhibits health when her members are "moving rhythmically and easily
with each other, efficient and graceful in response to God's Son, fully
mature adults, fully developed within and without, fully alive like
Christ." When the church is healthy, she dances!

When the church is healthy, she dances!

A compelling vision of the church will not only include an efficient
system but also a dynamic *relationship* among people who are whole in

25

Christ. The vision keeps the goal before us and helps us persevere during times of discouragement.

WHILE CHARLES CONTINUED to preach the priesthood of believers, I was benefiting from our church's awkward efforts to put the truth of Scripture into action. Even when applied awkwardly, God's truth carries life-changing power.

Charles realized that preaching about the priesthood of believers was important in order to lay a biblical foundation, but he was also going to have to involve more people. He called together a long-range planning committee. Nothing unnerves a group that worries about immediate survival more than someone who suggests thinking long-term. Charles met resistance. For one thing, some people told him that long-term planning sounded "unspiritual." Businesses did long-range planning, not churches.

Always alert for a teachable moment, Charles noted that planning is a significant part of the biblical view of life. Passages like James 4:13–17 ("What you ought to say is, 'If the Lord wants us to, we will live and do this or that'"—James 4:15 NLT) do not question the value of planning; they confront an attitude of carelessness about the future. Biblical planning seeks God's guidance and acknowledges God's essential role in implementing plans (see Proverbs 16:9; 19:21). It recognizes that God ultimately determines the success of any plan, and it rejects the notion that aiming at nothing is a spiritual practice.

Probably because he was still in the "honeymoon phase," Charles got some begrudging agreement to his suggestion that a long-range planning committee be formed. After all, people like me were getting the message about lay ministry, even if the practical application was still fuzzy. Charles displayed uncanny wisdom in the composition of the committee. The members represented a cross section of our church: young and old, married and single, new and old members, naysayers and progressives. Under Charles's direction they labored to discover the direction God had in mind for the church. For nine months they met biweekly to tackle tough questions like . . .

- Who is God calling us to be as a unique church within the larger body of Christ?
- Who is God calling us to be in this particular corner of West Los Angeles?
- Who is God calling us to be in this community of relative economic prosperity?

- Who is God calling us to be in the world?
- What are our resources in terms of people and finances?
- What are our limitations?

The questions were tough because they forced an existing group to question its reason to exist. The questions were uncomfortable because the answers were not immediately apparent. The group had to work hard, pray hard, study hard, and, above all, listen hard. They were learning to listen to each other—and to God as well.

One unexpected but crucial by-product of spending this time together was a deeper commitment to the vision by at least one small group in the church. Asking serious questions about the church's existence and purpose clarified the members' commitment to her. In time the long-range planning committee became comfortable with the idea that Charles was not going to let them go until their mission was accomplished. They began to own the vision.

Almost everyone in the congregation was learning the *language* of lay ministry, but the members of the long-range planning committee were gradually being filled with a *passion* for lay ministry. The important work they were doing on behalf of the entire church became our first model for the possibilities behind the vision: Laypeople in the body of Christ could plan strategically if given time, direction, and encouragement. Together they could experience a leading of God's Spirit that would result in practical connections between biblical teaching and the needs of the local church.

Almost everyone in the congregation was learning the *language* of lay ministry, but the members of the long-range planning committee were gradually being filled with a *passion* for lay ministry.

Gradually a plan took shape. One of its primary stated goals was to "transform our community." The rough idea included an affirmation of Charles's direction in preaching about the role of the laity and the significance of lay ministry, as well as a decision to find someone who could facilitate the expectation that each church member would find a place of service. The long-range planning committee realized that someone other than the pastor had to shepherd the process of change and oversee development of the new structures needed to implement the vision. The vision might be vivid, but if it wasn't going to move us to practical application, it would end up only as a memory.

MINISTER OF ENABLING

LOOKING BACK ON THE early days of our grand experiment, I'm humbled by how little we knew. We named this new position that I would fill "minister of enabling." We didn't realize how quickly cultural language could undermine our goals. Before I even began my work, the term *enabling* came to signify almost the exact opposite of what we intended it to mean. The recovery movement had adopted the word to explain the negative empowerment that can often function in unhealthy relationships. Almost overnight, *enabling* came to describe how a person allows and maybe even unwittingly helps another person to continue engaging in very destructive behaviors. Clearly this was not what we had in mind by our use of *enabling.*

This was only the first example of the significant task of education that awaited us. We wanted to free people to effectively minister. We wanted to help them help others toward wholeness, and we wanted to help people become more comfortable with change. And, in truth, I was not at all sure that my training justified the title "minister." So even before we launched the new ministry at Brentwood, we changed its name. I was to be the director of lay ministries.

In order for the new ministry concept to become rooted, it had to be accepted in the existing church culture, which in our case was Presbyterian. In that culture, even small changes must be processed and approved at many levels. Our governing board, called the Session, reviewed the work of the long-range planning committee and unanimously approved the plan. Next the vision was presented to the congregation at a dinner meeting. Maybe it was the drowsy aftereffects of a potluck or the contagious enthusiasm of the presenters, but there were few questions, and the congregation voted unanimously to approve the plan. Come to think of it, I probably should have taken that smooth trip through the legislative structure as a storm warning.

As soon as we began to implement the plan, walls of resistance rose like spring-loaded barriers in a pathway I had assumed was clear of obstacles. After all, we had voted! But once people realized that having a new organization and methodology for doing ministry meant a change in their personal way of "doing church," it became difficult to move forward. I not only discovered what it means to run into a brick wall, I found out that a wall sometimes falls on you when you run into it. People were enthusiastic about the idea of change until it affected them personally. I have since reached the settled conclusion that, of all the organizations I've ever worked with, the local church is most resistant to change, even when change has been the agreed plan.

**As soon as we began to implement the plan,
walls of resistance rose like spring-loaded barriers
in a pathway I had assumed was clear of obstacles.
After all, we had voted!**

The value of a clear biblical vision proved itself from the start. As important as it was to have formal congregational permission, the truth and power of the vision for lay ministry had already been rooted in our congregational thinking by Charles's faithful preaching of the core biblical texts: Romans 12:4–8, 1 Corinthians 12–14, and Ephesians 1–6. These provided our mandate. As long as we steered our decisions and actions by the guidance of these texts, we knew we were traveling under God's direction.

People were invited to find themselves in passages like Romans 12:4–8:

> Just as each of us has one body with many members, and these members do not all have the same function, so in Christ we who are many form one body, and each member belongs to all the others. We have different gifts, according to the grace given us. If a man's gift is prophesying, let him use it in proportion to his faith. If it is serving, let him serve; if it is teaching, let him teach; if it is encouraging, let him encourage; if it is contributing to the needs of others, let him give generously; if it is leadership, let him govern diligently; if it is showing mercy, let him do it cheerfully.

These verses were held up like a picture book of the body of Christ, as Charles asked us week after week, "Do you know your function? Are you doing it? Are we letting you do it? How can we better serve and support you?"

These last two questions helped define my own function in the body. It was my privilege to help all of us find and fulfill our own functions while letting others find theirs. But before I could begin to carry out my mission, I had to go through another unexpected training period. I began to discover what Charles had been realizing for several years— that having a clear and passionate vision doesn't make it happen in a group, even if you talk about it all the time. Other factors must be considered, or the "vision talk" will actually inoculate a group to the possibilities. Those were my next life lessons.

EQUIPPING PRINCIPLES

One Person Shares the Vision

The outline for the vision of the ministry of the people is found in Scripture. But this vision doesn't become reality until at least one person within the local church begins to "see" it. What they see is a dim outline of their own church taking on the shape and color of the biblical description. They begin to see not so much a building or a system, but an organism in which *each* part really does have a significant and meaningful function to perform. The biblical idea of the body of Christ makes no sense at all without the valued participation of the people.

Once one person begins to see the vision for lay ministry, the next step involves sharing the vision. This vision in particular must be shared with many before it can become a reality for all.

Senior Pastors Relinquish Control

As you will come to see, our pastor had to give up ownership of much of his previous work in ministry. He lost control, but he began to discover the principle Jesus taught when he spoke about the seed having to die before it brings forth fruit (see John 12:24). He eventually summarized the changes in his own role in these words: "This is so much about what I wanted to do when I entered the ministry that I shouldn't be paid to have this much fun!" You will also see as you read on that much of the transformation in our church can be traced to his preaching and his bold practicing of the vision long before the rest of us really understood it.

Teams Replace Committees

Significant differences exist between the mind-set of a team approach and the mind-set of committees. Although *committees* and *commitment* share linguistic roots, our culture in general does not equate serving on a committee with commitment. Committees tend to be highly leader centered. When a committee functions well, one of two things has usually happened: The leader is highly motivated to succeed and has done most of the work, or the committee has become a team. Committees can be transformed into teams by . . .

- doing the hard work of defining their purpose
- developing a role or responsibility for each person based on his or her gifts

- covenanting on how to work together and hold each other accountable
- coaching by the leader of the team
- effectively managing and delegating to appropriate team members
- becoming biblically centered and spiritually driven

A team is a group of uniquely gifted players with a common purpose. Each player has a responsibility and is given the authority to carry it out. As team members they are fully and jointly accountable to one another and to the team's results.

Speed Kills

At every point in our development of lay ministries there were always temptations to go faster. But we discovered (usually through our mistakes) that speeding up often slowed us down. As the old saying goes, whenever we thought we didn't have time to do it right, we ended up having to make time to do it again. A realistic timeline must be established and agreed on by all. Twelve to twenty-four months for seeing the vision start to take root is average, depending on many variables such as size of the church, leadership skills, care-team development, and the church's starting point.

Shortcuts Are Often Dead Ends

As you read our story, remember that your experience in lay ministry will be different. Your circumstances are not the same as ours (I can't say that often enough). But also remember this: The key components we've discovered have been regularly discovered by others. As more and more Christians from diverse backgrounds compare their stories and their discoveries in lay-driven churches, the more we see striking similarities with respect to some essential insights. If you are tempted to take a shortcut around some of the principles of healthy lay ministry, we can promise you some dead ends. Depending on the size of your church, you may have to blend some of the components, but please don't leave any out. Their absence may well cause the whole vision to collapse.

EQUIPPING HEROES

Grace Community Church
Noblesville, Indiana
www.gracecc.org
Senior Pastor: Dave Rodriguez

Adaptability and willingness to change are key factors to stay-ing in the game. Grace Community Church places a high value on excellence, equipping her leaders (both paid and nonpaid), and being an equipping church in every aspect. What is exceptional about this church is how they apply what they are learning to the felt needs of leaders and church members. I dare say many of us attend conferences as a team and talk through the things we've learned, but then we go home and get right back to business as usual because we are too busy to make the changes that would enhance our ministries.

Not so at Grace. After attending two conferences in 1999 (the Willow Creek "Leadership Summit" and Leadership Training Net-work's "New Century: New Church") and being exposed to a new principle for leadership and reproducing leaders taught by Wayne Cordeiro, senior pastor at New Hope Christian Fellowship in Oahu, Hawaii, this team took application seriously. The fact that they had critical needs enabled them to hear God's plan for change in their church through the experiences of another church.

Before boarding the plane after the second conference had ended, the team from Grace Community met for several hours. The staff solicited the lay leaders' reaction and input, both positive and negative. The most important response they heard was the concern that their church was hiring ministry to be done rather than empow-ering church members to be the ministers. So the staff resolved to chart a path for change, celebrating the successes and owning the feelings and frustrations of the lay leaders.

For the last year Grace Community has lived through the chaotic process of restructuring staff and reproducing leaders based on the church's values, passion, giftedness, and community. *Fractaling* (defined as a pattern that infinitely repeats itself throughout an organism) is the buzzword and known by all! See Wayne Cordeiro's book *Doing Church as a Team* (a great resource for your equipping library) for an in-depth explanation of how fractaling can be used to grow leaders and the ministry of the church.

Grace Community Church has always placed a high value on people and community connections—on doing what is best for the body. Through restructuring the staff and all the processes for ministry and leadership development, the church is moving toward her vision of helping people see themselves as kingdom players. Is it perfect? Not by a long shot. Is it easy? Not in the least. It is a work in progress filled with challenges, but for leaders who genuinely have a heart for people and a desire to be part of an equipping church that truly serves the kingdom, all things are possible.

First United Methodist Church
www.fumcbixby.org
Bixby, Oklahoma
Senior Pastor: Jessica Moffatt

Jessica made the transition from being executive pastor at a large United Methodist congregation in Tulsa, Oklahoma (after twelve years in mobilizing ministry), to senior pastor at a small United Methodist church with a uniquely different culture, just a few miles away. She recognized that mass identification of everyone's gifts was not the way to proceed, and so she wisely started with "roundtable theology," whether at a three hundred-member table or a five-member staff table. She emphasized the principle of "different functions, equal importance." She described her function in the body and then lifted up the need and equality of every person around whatever table at which she was seated.

Jessica's approach created a climate of mutual discovery, studying Scripture together to discern God's design for the church and each person's role rather than having the pastor dictate whatever seemed correct to him or her. This was a surprise to her new church family and certainly a departure from the role of a traditional UMC pastor. Vital to her success as a leader was the insistence that each member was of equal importance—a truth she had to model first.

Jessica quickly perceived that the well-tuned system of her previous megachurch would not work in this church, so together they created a new model that was compatible with the needs of the culture at Bixby. Roadblocks were encountered along the way, such as the traditional expectations of what a senior pastor ought to be, as well as some people's resistance to seeing themselves as the ministers (*you* are the minister; I'm not!). Defining their culture as a "casserole community" that meets life transitions with food and a ministry of caring presence, Jessica and her team recognized that they simply had to come up with some new casserole recipes.

Bixby is a loving, thoughtful community that places a high value on caring for people. Like many churches the first shift in Bixby's culture involved language. They had to fashion a language for ministry that was accurate biblically and culturally. They asked themselves the crucial question, "Does our language reflect the church of Jesus Christ?" If it does, they are taking a significant step forward in helping people understand that they are a royal priesthood, that they must all be players in the equipping church.

A closing thought: It's important to note that what works well in one congregation will not necessarily work in another. The wise leader reads, understands, and respects the culture, and then adapts the learning process to reach the end goal.

QUESTIONS FOR REFLECTION AND DISCUSSION

1. What is your vision-casting process? Do you have a long-range plan? How does your plan identify equipping ministry as a priority for transformation and growth?

2. Does your church have a designated staff position to facilitate equipping ministry?

3. Where are the walls of resistance in your church?

4. How would you define your church's readiness for change?

Making Systemic Changes Can Be Shocking

It was he who gave some to be apostles, some to be prophets, some to be evangelists, and some to be pastors and teachers, to prepare God's people for works of service, so that the body of Christ may be built up until we all reach unity in the faith and in the knowledge of the Son of God and become mature, attaining to the whole measure of the fullness of Christ.

Ephesians 4:11–13

HOW EASY IT IS to focus on the descriptions Paul gives in Ephesians 4 and mistake them as simply positions—apostles, prophets, evangelists, pastors, and teachers. For a long time they sounded to me like official designations. Then I discovered that these are *serving* roles. I had almost unconsciously assumed they were rungs on the ladder of spiritual success. My assumptions were shattered when I looked carefully at how the Bible speaks of the church. In biblical practice these descriptive labels often affirmed a role someone was already carrying out. Someone was called an evangelist because she was already exercising the gift of evangelism; someone else was affirmed as an apostle because he was carrying out apostolic functions in the church.

When we yield to the temptation to establish ranks and esteem prestige within the body of Christ, we promote disunity and envy of place. When I tried to discern an order of importance in this list, I ended up sounding like the whispered argument among Jesus' disciples about which of them was the greatest. Jesus interrupted my internal discussion with these words: "If anyone wants to be first, he must be the very last, and the servant of all" (Mark 9:35).

Ultimately a church's faithfulness can be measured by this question: To what degree does each member understand herself or himself to be connected to Christ and accountable to him for the way they live and serve? Someone has to ask this question and serve the church by keeping it in front of everyone else. In our church I was offered that life-changing privilege.

THRILLED BUT TERRIFIED

WHEN CHARLES INFORMED ME that the church's leaders had agreed to call me to be the director of lay ministries, I was thrilled but terrified. We had discussed the possibility in some detail as I was recovering from surgery. He knew I had been hugely affected by the care I had received from other church members and understood my desire to see to it that others got the same kind of care. But I wasn't sure I was ready for the "whole enchilada" (to use good Southern California talk). Charles affirmed my love for people and my desire to connect them to each other and to God. I knew that great things were possible if the church could connect members to one another in loving, caring community and intentionally unleash people for service.

When Charles and I looked at the job description, it listed a lot of things I had no experience in—computer skills, for instance. But I knew enough to respond to my limitations with two standard answers: I can learn, and better yet, I can invite someone else to lead in those areas. From day one I resolved to broaden the base of ministry by supplementing my lack of skill and experience with the people who had the right gifts. I did this with the full blessing of my pastor.

One strength I brought to the job was a passion for service and care. Charles decided to base his support for my role on those character traits. From the start we both placed a high value on inviting the greatest number of people to join in the ministry of service.

Although the church had approved funding for the job, I chose to serve as nonpaid staff. I was surprised that this was to become a point of conflict. I experienced firsthand one of the complications that come from using money as a primary measurement of and point of accountability for legitimate ministry (see the equipping principle on page 47). Pay was not the issue for me. Serving was my way of giving back in gratitude for what my family and I had received from the community of faith. In my naïveté I initiated some great learning opportunities for the whole church. We discussed some of the hidden barriers to trusting, equipping, and managing church members who are not formally employed by the church.

When I responded to my pastor's offer, he gave me a revealing set of instructions, which included requiring a weekly accountability meeting with him. Beyond that, I was required to define the role and to live the goals and objectives set forth by the long-range plan. Only upon later reflection did I realize that I had been given little direction on how to succeed, leaving me with a rather large potential for failure. The position of director of lay ministries (as is true of practically every position in the church) came with high expectations and low specifics. My experiences in other church settings over the years have taught me this indelible lesson: The church by definition is the greatest gathering of potential servants in the world, but she is also the most notorious vehicle for disappointing, discouraging, and even destroying them. Only a small percentage of willing volunteers can succeed without specific training and clear direction—and the church seldom offers either. Addressing this failure became one of my primary goals.

The church by definition is the greatest gathering of potential servants in the world, but she is also the most notorious vehicle for disappointing, discouraging, and even destroying them.

When I said yes to the job of director of lay ministries, I signed up for another season of helplessness. This role was so new that it had no form. The title acknowledged a need, but no one told me how to meet it. When I accepted the position, I was eager to do something helpful, but I quickly found out I had a lot to learn before I could do any effective directing of lay ministries.

EIGHTEEN MONTHS UNDERGROUND

A LOCAL CHURCH FUNCTIONS as a system. People within the system operate like interlocking gears inside of a complex machine. Turn any gear in the system, and all the others move in some way. We clearly had a working system at Brentwood, but we knew it could do a better job reflecting more closely the biblical description of the church.

Since I began my work convinced that my role was needed, it came as quite a shock to realize that my actual participation in the system was often not wanted. People who had reported real dissatisfaction with the way things were going were some of the first to tell me that any suggestions I had or changes I made ought to be done elsewhere.

It took me (with the help of a committed team) eighteen months to figure out what to do and how to do it, and then to start doing it. When I talk with church leaders today about the kind of systemic changes that equipping ministry requires in a church, I find that one of the greatest stumbling blocks is the length of time it takes to build or enhance a system. I now know that my experience represents the average time frame for a setting in which a good deal of healthy groundwork has already been completed. I've shared the frustration of many who have nurtured agonizing change, only to be told that their efforts are unacceptable; I've cried with those who have been informed by their church that this kind of change will not be accepted, no matter how long they work at it. Sadly, in some places the vision of genuine lay ministry will be rejected.

During the first of those eighteen months I survived on the bare conviction that the vision of an equipping church was biblical—that it was, in fact, true. That, along with my weekly meetings with my pastor, carried me until the vision began to take root. Charles didn't know enough about the job to tell me what to do, but he was wise enough to encourage me to discover what it was that I needed to do. The need to report weekly compelled me to keep at it, even during discouraging times.

I remember being impressed by Charles's reluctance to spell out the job for me. I assumed it was a crafty technique for forcing me to exercise my own gifts and creativity in shaping the role. Years later, after he heard me give him credit for this amazing and patient approach to the ministry, he sheepishly confessed, "I took that approach out of sheer ignorance, Sue. I really didn't know how your role would work, but I knew if I asked you enough questions, if I encouraged and supported you enough, you would find it out. My role was to keep asking you questions long enough for you to figure out how we could make the vision come alive."

Charles was unknowingly practicing a very effective method we've come to call "management by I don't know." It's significantly different from "management by I don't care"; it's not abdication of leadership. Traditionally people have expected their pastors to be the knowers and the doers of all significant things, which puts them in virtually impossible situations and often sets them up for failure. In truth, leaders do not *have* to know or do everything. They have to care about, advocate for, and support those who know what needs to be known and who can do the things that need to be done. And they have to surround themselves with people who, though they may not know at the moment, can go and find out. When neither Charles nor I had a clue what to do next, he patiently waited for me to find out.

Well, as time went on I did find out. God provided some unexpected and wonderful guides along the way, and my helplessness was transformed once again into a sense of hopefulness. As the vision took on a specific shape that made sense for our particular church, new systems were created, albeit over the course of many months, to allow us to support the vision.

A JOB WITHOUT TRAINING

ALTHOUGH THE CHURCH had asked me to perform a valuable function that had clear biblical support, other support seemed nonexistent. I began to look for help but couldn't find any churches that were doing what we were trying to do. Training opportunities abounded, but none seemed to fit our situation. Although the church growth movement was in full bloom, I couldn't find any concentrated training designed to improve church health.

Almost by accident I stumbled upon a group called DOVIA (Directors of Volunteers in Agencies), a nationwide organization that provides support for directors of nonprofit organizations. I began to meet with Red Cross directors, food bank coordinators, and heads of hospital volunteer programs. I was introduced to a previously hidden world of experienced people who had developed a wealth of training in effective ways to manage volunteers.

As excited as I was about everything I was learning, I realized that my true challenge would be to evaluate these techniques according to scriptural standards and to translate the right ones into a language and format that would fit or transform our systems within the church. My goal became to learn the lessons of volunteerism and then to take the biblical application into the Christ-centered ministry of the church.

My association with DOVIA led directly to the Association for Volunteer Administration (AVA), a group that provides national and international standards and oversight for members of DOVIA and other volunteer groups. In 1986 I attended my first international AVA conference. I joined nine hundred highly motivated leaders who were managing volunteers in a dizzying variety of settings. My biggest shock came when I discovered that I was the only person on the roster who directed volunteers in a faith community. How could I be the only official church representative when faith communities corporately have by far the largest number of volunteers in the United States?

My concern was soon overshadowed by the myriad of opportunities that awaited me. I remember thinking that I must have wandered into heaven. The AVA conference seemed to offer absolutely everything

---

> **My biggest shock came when I discovered
> I was the only person on the roster who directed
> volunteers in a faith community.**

---

anyone could ever want to know about volunteer management. I was overwhelmed by the choices: seminars on burnout, conflict resolution, recruitment, recognition, and many others—one after another. Frantically I went all out to avoid missing anything. All the while questions kept echoing through my mind: How would this work in our church? Do we need to know this? Every volunteer management skill and principle had to meet certain criteria to pass biblical muster. Could I illustrate and teach them from the Scriptures? Would they fit into our present system (denominational structure and local church system), or would they have to wait until the system changed? These questions became my primary evaluation grid. The beauty of this time for me was that it forced me to think carefully about my understanding of the church. I certainly had to reevaluate my own direction, objectives, and job description—and through it all it was a time of great personal growth.

A TITLE WITHOUT A PLACE

NOT LONG AFTER I became director of lay ministries, I experienced a growing sense of uneasiness in my weekly interactions with my pastor. When I asked Charles about this, he readily confessed to a measure of awkwardness in knowing how to treat me. At first I wasn't sure what the problem was, but after a period of time Charles finally said, "I guess I don't know how to deal with you as a volunteer. How can I hold you accountable? We don't pay you to do this ministry, so I find it hard to hold you to the same standards I would expect from a paid staff person."

We had stumbled upon a blind spot in our system and values. Actually, we had uncovered a lethal assumption about laypeople, money, and accountability. We were carrying on the time-honored error of equating pay with "real ministry" as opposed to unpaid "semiministry." What's more, we were assuming that we could expect someone to keep their word if we were paying them, but without a paycheck commitments would invariably be less binding.

I call this a lethal assumption because I'm convinced it kills pastoral ministry and discourages a great deal of lay ministry. Pastors end up taking on all kind of roles and tasks, even if they're ill equipped to perform them, simply because they accept the understanding that "it's what they pay me for!" Meanwhile, laypeople sometimes shy away from ministry that they're well equipped to do simply because they're afraid they'll be stepping on the pastor's toes. The pastor went to seminary, so surely he or she is able to do "all things!" Or, what's worse, laypeople volunteer to undertake a project, only to be told that because there's no money to pay them, the project will have to wait. When it comes to receiving pay for ministry, need and circumstance should be the highest priority in evaluating salary levels. A paycheck does not automatically make one person's ministry more worthy or valuable than another person with similar gifts who does his or her ministry without receiving pay.

We were carrying on the time-honored error of equating pay with "real ministry" as opposed to unpaid "semiministry."

Because Charles and I were both committed to a larger vision, we knew we couldn't let this issue derail us. I simply told him to pretend that he was paying me and leave it at that until we had worked out the relationship. The truth is, if we couldn't get beyond this, we wouldn't be able to do the more significant work of changing the system itself.

OLD SYSTEM/NEW SYSTEM INTERFACE

SIGNIFICANT CHANGES SOMETIMES produce shocks. I unknowingly created one the first time I joined the weekly staff meeting. Here I was, a layperson, rushing in where only staff dared to tread. On the one hand, I had a title and a place in the church structure—director of lay ministries; on the other, I held the position as an unpaid staff member, a first for our church. So which of those facts would determine whether or not I had a seat at the table in the staff meeting?

What a delicious dilemma! These awkward occasions and their resolutions really help determine the depth of commitment in a church to the principle of lay ministry. If we don't believe laypeople can do real ministry, we will naturally exclude them from staff discussions about the ministry. But if we passionately believe that laypeople are gifted and equipped by God for every kind of ministry, then we will insist that they be represented in any discussion of ministry. Needless to say, I began attending all staff meetings with Charles's blessing, but I had to earn my right to be there.

The first lessons I brought back from my training outside the church walls focused on awareness and tracking. We said we wanted to be a church that encouraged the ministry of the laity and equipped them for it—how well did we know what was going on among our people? Who was already doing what, and what kind of success were they having? My enthusiasm for tracking was met by the staff with sobering skepticism. My first mistake was probably using the word *tracking*. Our minister of music, Jack Walker, shared what others in the group were thinking as well. Speaking from his tender ministerial heart he said, "I just don't want to do tracking. It's too corporate. I'm not going have my choir members be numbers. There's enough of that in the business world." As he and others voiced their resistance, I realized I had shot myself in the foot. (It wasn't the first or the last time either—it's a small miracle that I can still walk!) I hadn't used language that communicated ministry values—and I had learned a priceless lesson.

A week later I experimented with another approach. I asked my pastor for a moment at a staff meeting to address an area of ministry. Since I had been active in the choir for several years, I began my experiment with Jack and the choir, a fairly large group in our church. During the "concerns" portion of the staff meeting, I said, "Jack, I haven't seen Beverly lately. Is she ill? I've noticed she hasn't sung with the choir for at least a couple of weeks." Jack said, "You know, you're right. I haven't seen her either." I then mentioned two or three other people I noticed had been missing in his ministry area, and I surrendered the floor.

The next week as the staff gathered Jack made a point of saying to me in that public setting, "Sue, I'm so glad you mentioned Beverly to me last week. She's been out with a terrible bout of flu. If you hadn't alerted me, I would have missed an opportunity to minister to her." His comment provided a perfect opportunity to begin a dialogue in which I mentioned several more names—in someone else's ministry area this time. And on it went. For the next six weeks, in each staff meeting I came armed with a short list of names of people active in different areas of ministry whose absence I had been noticing. By the end of those six weeks there was a measurable personalizing of our ministry as staff members were calling people and discovering needs that might otherwise have gone unmet. In our staff meetings others began mentioning noticed absentees as well.

During one of those meetings I launched phase two of my plan by saying, "I'm certainly learning how easy it is to overlook absentees. What if we could find a way to improve our awareness of people's needs in the congregation? What if we made a more intentional effort to know who's here and who's not? Do you think we could improve our ministry by knowing people better?"

What came next were sweet words of permission, the lowering of the guard, as someone asked, "Do you have any ideas how we could do this, Sue?"

Did I have ideas? Well, one word had come immediately to my mind: *computer*. I figured while I had their attention, I might as well aim high. I was bluffing. You have to understand that I was personally way out of my league at this point. I could talk the computer talk but couldn't walk the computer walk, nor could I type the computer type. I was keyboard illiterate and cyber-challenged at that time.

They called my bluff and told me to develop a tracking system. I began by reviewing what we actually had in the way of congregational information. What I found was not encouraging. We had no organized, centralized method for gathering, storing, or sharing information about the members of the congregation. Fortunately, though, my complete inadequacy in the area of computers became the doorway for a number of people to practice their passion in a brand-new ministry.

The starting point proved to be a relationship I had developed in another area of ministry. My choir participation had included sharing a ride with Bruce, whose vocation involved training people with disabilities in the use of computers. Legally blind himself, Bruce had a unique gift for helping people who faced severe challenges become capable computer users. I was amazed at what he did, even though I didn't understand much of it. As we rode together, he heard a week-by-week review of my experiences in my new role as director of lay ministries. One evening I asked, "Bruce, would you help me figure out how we could use computers to gather, store, and apply all kinds of information to improve our ministry as a church?"

Bruce responded without hesitation, "I would love to do that!" He became the leader and first member of my computer team. I asked if he could suggest other people to enlist in this effort, and he told me he'd get back to me. It wasn't long before Bruce had identified eight people who had significant abilities in the area of computers, and we invited them to form a team. For some of them it was the first time they had been asked to do something in a church setting for which they were already trained and equipped. An area that terrified me was their home turf. They were actually excited about what they might be able to do for the church. I told them what we needed, and they answered, "No problem!" Their exuberance was contagious. They made me believe they could turn our dreams into data.

The computer team set out to review the kinds of programs available on the market. At the same time they contacted other churches and nonprofit groups for ideas. They scoured the marketplace, but they came up with nothing that would meet our specific needs. To my amazement, this bad news actually energized them. Now they wouldn't have to adapt someone else's stuff. They were going to build our program from the ground up.

They made me believe they could turn our dreams into data.

Bruce managed the team that created the database that marked the beginning of our equipping ministry system. Bruce helped me see that sometimes an equipping church does her best work when she unleashes people who are already equipped so they can do a special work of ministry.

Setting up the original system was frustrating and time-consuming, but it was an integral part of the foundation of change that supports our values. We got the right people to do the right project, and they did it the right way! As the results of their efforts came to light, we knew that our church was experiencing transformation. But alongside changes in the system, other basic needs had to be addressed as well. Our church represented a culture that needed to be understood too. The most effective system in the world would be little more than a pile of computer chips if the existing church culture failed to be accounted for in the new understanding of the church.

EQUIPPING PRINCIPLES

Change Your Language to Reflect Biblical Values

The chart below provides some examples of the kinds of shifts in language that will promote and reinforce the mind-set of ministry and transformation. Identifying the language you presently use and evaluating its effectiveness can be both challenging and fun. Experiment with changes. Make sure that people understand the language you are using and the message you are conveying, and don't forget to connect the language with the culture in which you all live.

SECULAR MENTALITY	MINISTRY MENTALITY
Do you?	Or do you?
delegate	share ministry
fill slots	identify ministry opportunities
use job descriptions	use ministry descriptions
call people volunteers	call people ministers, unpaid servants, servant leaders, saints
have committees	serve on teams

Not all these language shifts are obvious. Most of them, however, are necessary. The equipping vision requires that a church's organizing language change to recognize the biblical value that sees each believer as a minister, or to put it another way, that affirms the priesthood of all believers.

Analyze the Present System

People in a church can function without consciously recognizing the systems that shape their decisions and their life together as part of a community of believers. To be an equipping church you will have to learn to ask the right questions. Your primary tool will be your capacity to observe and your willingness to invite others to observe with you. Here are some key system-analysis questions to ask:

- How do we know who is part of this church?
- How do people become part of this church?
- What happens to people until they become part of this church?
- What happens to people *after* they commit to membership?
- What are the stated membership requirements?
- How are people held accountable to their membership covenants?
- What are the lines of accountability within the church? Who answers to whom?

Allow Time to Get There

I wasn't prepared for the amount of time it would take to implement even the simplest system change. Declaring something changed and having it *act* changed were often two very different things. We spent eighteen months underground just to launch the new way of doing ministry at Brentwood. At that point we had already come a good distance from where we had begun, but we had a long, long way to go.

Look for Validation from the Senior Pastor and Staff

We did at least one thing right at Brentwood from the start— even though we didn't realize at the time how right it was. Our grand adventure in ministry had the full, enthusiastic, intentional, and persistent support of the senior pastor. I have come to see this as one of the nonnegotiable factors in promoting genuine change and effective transformation of church culture.

Though I have been invited to cast the vision for an equipping church at large church gatherings convened to explore the transition to a fully functioning mobilized church, I've had to decline on more than one occasion. Why? Because of my strong conviction that the absence of the senior pastor and the lack of clear support from existing leadership meant that the group's efforts would be derailed from the outset.

Recognize and Value "Management by I Don't Know"

As I've stated above (see page 38), "management by I don't know" (Charles also called it "management by muddling through") is strikingly different from "management by I don't care." The principle behind the method seems to come as an eye-opener to both senior pastors and most church members. Both groups often accept without much thought the idea that the pastor knows all, sees all, does all. I've talked with people who sheepishly admitted that they've treated their pastor as if part of the service of ordination had included his taking on the attribute of omniscience!

"Management by I don't know" affirms the following for the pastor: There are many crucial decisions, actions, and ministries that I have neither the ability nor the time to carry out, but they still need doing. Let's invite someone to do it! "Management by I don't care" is the old stereotype of know-all, see-all, do-all in subtle disguise, and it affirms the following for the pastor: Since I know and do everything that really matters, if I don't know or can't do something, then it must not really matter!

Like parents who are honest about their strengths and weaknesses when it comes to rearing their children, pastors who admit their gift and training limitations and invite others to share in ministry do not lose the admiration of others—except, of course, of those they wouldn't be able to please no matter how much they did!

Learn to Trust Lay Leaders to Make Wise Decisions

The pastor who validates lay ministry is not diminished in value or role. We discovered that Charles's pastoral roles in many ways were highlighted as he encouraged others to do pieces of the overall ministry he hadn't been equipped to do but had inherited as part of pastoral expectations.

The fear lurking behind discussions of giving laypeople significant decision-making authority in church is that they don't know enough or are not committed enough to make wise decisions. And yet, churches do not function without some level of congregational decision making. Laypeople sometimes do make poor decisions—and so do pastors. Those who have come to the point of consistently making good decisions have usually learned through the experiences of making bad decisions. A church that makes an intentional decision to train her members into wise leaders who are capable of making good decisions has taken a significant step toward becoming an equipping church.

What's more, people commit to the decisions they help make—both with their dollars and their time.

Adopt a Proper Perspective on Money

While we may not like it, money questions lie hidden behind most serious conversations about lay ministry. An argument can easily break out over comparisons between the "ministry of the paid" and the "ministry of the unpaid." These issues are rarely settled by using an "either/or" framework. The apostle Paul provides a good example of the "both/and." Was Paul doing more effective ministry when he received financial support from other believers or when he earned his own way as a tentmaker?

The practical discoveries we've made at Brentwood after more than a decade of serious commitment to this ministry have led us to several conclusions:

- Financial compensation can facilitate or complicate ministry, but it cannot validate ministry. Big budgets don't automatically translate to effective or even required ministry; little budgets don't either.
- Ministry done by laypeople isn't necessarily cheap.
- Ministry done by paid staff isn't necessarily expensive.

Money should be low on the list of measurements in evaluating ministry. More important are such issues as . . .

- Biblical mandate: Has God led us or told us to do this? God never provides a financial loophole with his commands. Directives like feed the hungry and clothe the naked don't include a parenthetical (unless it's too expensive) excuse.
- Priority: With respect to all the needs facing us, is this particular ministry receiving the proper amount of attention and energy?
- Resource use: How well are we using what we already have?—not, How can we get more?
- Dollar values: Does our budget reflect what we say we value?

Exercise Equality among Believers

As I'll make clear later, one of the central issues in a church that acknowledges the priesthood of believers and shared ministry of the people is the obvious (and sometimes subtle) practice of equality among believers. This is so much more than making glowing verbal statements about the value of laypeople. Are the gifts of the laity celebrated with the same warmth as the gifts of the ordained are? Perhaps they shouldn't be celebrated in exactly the same way, but are they celebrated at all?

How does a church appropriately recognize someone who has graciously and effectively ministered as the second grade Sunday school teacher for a couple of decades and touched the life of every person who has grown up in the church? Does the handyman who donates his time and extraordinary talent ever receive a thoughtful expression of gratitude from those whom he or she has served, albeit in perhaps a rather subtle way? How do we intentionally seek to help each member sense their significance within the body?

Don't Let the Appearance of Chaos Distract You

Perhaps as you read this chapter, you found yourself muttering over and over, "Sue, our church is an exception. We don't have a tracking or communication system. We have chaos!" If so, I invite you to consider these possibilities:

- Where chaos reigns, I find that a system is usually trying to take or maintain control.
- Chaos may mean that two or more systems are in competition.
- Chaos may indicate a dysfunctional system crying out for change.
- Chaos may result when a past effective system has been gradually overwhelmed and routed by other change factors (community changes, relationship conflicts, or leadership disasters).

Don't let the appearance of chaos distract you from observing, analyzing, and enhancing your present system.

Recognize That Tracking Doesn't Necessarily Put You On Track

Having a sophisticated system for gathering exhaustive information on everyone remotely connected to the church means little as an end in itself. The way you gather that information and what you do with it make all the difference.

People want to be cared for, not targeted. We discovered, and I'm sure you will too, that people need to be assured that the information you gain from or about them will not be used against them. By the same token, those involved in gathering information provide in the very process some of the most valuable ministry within a church. People often receive affirmation of their gifts from the interaction with those who interview them.

Don't Expect Perfection

When I tell the Brentwood story at seminars in which I'm participating, I often have to correct the impression that we have a perfect system that yields flawless results. Here's the truth. We never even aimed at perfection. When we started our adventure, we figured that we had about 10 percent significant participation and about 90 percent incidental participation by congregational members in the life of the church. We wanted to reverse the trend and hopefully approach 80 percent involvement and 20 percent passivity among our people. We felt this was a good objective for several reasons:

- At any given time in church life, some people will be in transition between specific functions.
- At any given time in church life, some people will have needs and struggles that place them primarily in a dependent role with respect to the church. Those whom we serve during times when they cannot reciprocate will often become some of the most active contributors later on.
- We live in a fallen world. Some in any congregation will simply refuse to participate beyond the bare minimum. They may not be ideal members, but they certainly provide ample opportunity for the practice of unconditional love.

EQUIPPING HEROES

Lake Pointe Baptist Church
Rockwall, Texas
www.lakepointe.org
Senior Pastor: Steve Stroope
Director of Ministry Involvement: Brandon Tidwell

Senior pastor Steve Stroope recognizes that systems and clear processes allow the church to pursue excellence in all areas of ministry. Steve has long valued the equipping church and was part of the start-up dream team that envisioned what was to become Leadership Training Network.

When Brandon Tidwell was called to the role of director of ministry involvement at Lake Pointe, he spent most of his first year assessing the foundational systems that were already in place and significant systems that were lacking. He found the greatest need in the area of assimilation.

As an empowering leader/coach, Brandon formed an outstanding team of gifted leaders to address the need. Each took a piece of the large puzzle to create an exceptional assimilation process, unique and customized to the culture and structure of Lake Pointe, a church that was being led in and through the Adult Bible Fellowship (ABF) model. After assessing all that was out there, the team created a discovery process unique to their needs (based in large part on Mels Carbonell's *Uniquely You* giftedness profiles). They couldn't find what they needed in the way of software, so through the gifts and passions of the team, they adapted and created until they had software that was effective in their particular structure.

The leaders at Lake Pointe decentralized the assimilation process by means of the Adult Bible Fellowship groups and shaped needed systems to gather and disseminate information for that model. They trained the leaders of the ABF groups in the newly created process for assimilation and discovery and allowed uniqueness in the process—even within each group. They did not try to get the church to change shape without a reason. They wisely conformed to existing structures and set them up to succeed within the immediate culture. They centralized the information but decentralized the process of gathering and sharing the communications.

Of all the models I've seen, Lake Pointe exemplifies especially well the understanding that systems exist to serve the people. The lay ministry team members went out of their way not only to serve those they were trying to discover but also, equally important, the leaders who would collaborate in the process. Lake Pointe is, without apology, a church of systems that support spiritual growth, fellowship, care, ministry videos, newsletters, job descriptions, assimilation, and on and on. They are serving their people well.

> Willow Creek Community Church
> South Barrington, Illinois
> www.willowcreek.org
> Senior Pastor: Bill Hybels
> Director of Ministry Services: Marge Anderson

Marge Anderson has an unbridled passion for God's people. She brought valuable insights to her job as a result of having served as a volunteer in several different ministries in the church. She saw firsthand the wounds and disappointments of people who had slipped through the cracks or had never been equipped to serve in the area where they had been placed. Marge had an agenda: to ensure that people did not fall through the cracks and to be a good steward of people resources. She was driven both by her own passion and by the needs of others.

"Messing around" in one ministry area at a time, building relationships and trust, Marge helped solve problems by setting up systems that would serve each particular ministry. One by one she found the felt needs and met them through systems that provided excellent support, proper placement, and timely follow-through. Marge made her greatest impact in small group ministry, as the connections began to increase and take root. Her love and care for people was the driver for systems to serve, nurture, and protect them. She had a passion for the end result (people) but knew the process had to be in place in order to make the passion come alive.

Marge helped decentralize the process by assigning ministry assimilators to every ministry. These assimilators meet together monthly to discuss tracking issues, to share best practices—invitations that worked well, things that seem to be "mission impossible," such as voice mails, and the like—and to think outside the box and dream. The regular meetings provide accountability, evaluation of what's working and insight into how to make it even better, and opportunities to share stories of the heart, where lives are being transformed. In addition to reporting on ministry progress, the assimilators receive regular training on such things as how to listen well, identify ministry passions, and engage in evangelism.

The process of moving from the conception of Marge's vision to being fully valued and supported with the necessary resources took between two and three years; the team model necessary to support the systemic needs of the church was taking root during that time as well, until it reached its full function after a period of five to six years.

Willow Creek Community Church is a church of systems, to be sure, but for the most part these systems are invisible. The best ones always are! The purpose of an efficient system is to accomplish a goal, not necessarily to be seen. And we all know that a broken system ends up drawing attention to itself.

Willow Creek has created an equipping culture modeled from the top down. They have developed and continually adjust systems to facilitate ministries. Systems can intentionally change lives. The volunteers at the church are known and valued because the teaching pastors constantly preach and teach the value of people—and that value becomes contagious! People own it in their own way. Marge, whose life has been deeply affected by others at the church, told me she has "a purified passion for making our church function well so that people can be enfolded." I know from the way she said it that she personally experienced it!

QUESTIONS FOR REFLECTION AND DISCUSSION

1. Do you pay staff to "do ministry" or to equip and unleash people?

2. How would your staff embrace and respond to a non-paid staff member?

3. Does your information system simply track data, or does it track ministry opportunities to serve and be served?

4. What systems do you have in place to assimilate people, connect people into ministry, and follow through with the connection?

Examining, Poking, and Prodding the Church Culture

He handed out gifts of apostle, prophet, evangelist, and pastor-teacher to train Christians in skilled servant work, working within Christ's body, the church, until we're all moving rhythmically and easily with each other, efficient and graceful in response to God's Son, fully mature adults, fully developed within and without, fully alive like Christ.

Ephesians 4:11–13 THE MESSAGE

WHEN I BRING THE idea of *culture* to Ephesians 4:11–13, I find some important principles at work. Whereas the systems in a church are designed to apply the "doing" words in these verses, the culture seeks to bring meaning to the "being" words. I've noticed that each church culture seems to develop a specific understanding of the following words: gifts, apostle, prophet, evangelist, pastor-teacher, Christian, servant, church, adults. We may or may not know how the Bible defines each of these "being" words—but we do know how our denomination or local church uses them. Why? Because it's our church culture.

While some churches assign all the above terms to their members, many churches highlight only a couple. In some church cultures, terms like "apostle" and "prophet" have been semiretired—they are only used to describe gifts that God once gave to the church but no longer exist. Some terms ("evangelist" and "servant," for instance) are studiously ignored. Some roles receive more honor and recognition than others. Some are temporarily assigned to laypeople, while others are reserved as lifelong titles for those who officially minister among the laity.

While systems are often written down (just look at the abundance of books of discipline and rules of order), cultures tend to be passed down through relationships. (Another way to put it is this: Systems are in books and cultures are in looks.) While reading the published "organizational chart" of leadership positions in a church will tell you about the system, asking a question at a congregational meeting and observing the one toward whom all heads turn will tell you about the power flow in the culture. Systems can often be analyzed from the outside; cultures must be understood from the inside. Healthy and wise change rarely happens apart from deep cultural understanding. Christ's gifts of people (and the gifts he gives to people) can change the church from the inside out. Systems, good and bad, offer a structured description of what we are trying to do; the culture is who we are and what we *actually* do. Though systems and culture are not identical, they must work in harmony. When they cooperate and support one another, healthy growth, positive change, and transformed lives are all possible.

EXAMINING, POKING, AND PRODDING THE CHURCH CULTURE

IN THE LAST CHAPTER I described some of the system changes we went through early on at Brentwood. You probably noticed that more was involved than just describing, evaluating, and changing church structures. Some of those structures were not subject to change. What we didn't need to do was abandon our Presbyterian roots or traditions; in fact, in some ways we had to pay more attention to them. Our church heritage, like many of yours, developed over centuries of trial and error by faithful men and women who struggled to express the eternal values of the gospel in the situations in which they found themselves. By and large they succeeded admirably. Since they passed on a legacy that includes the eternal truth of God, our own faithfulness will be measured to a large extent by our success in preserving that core of truth in the changing world in which we live.

We were not just *creating* change, for change was inevitable. We were doing our best to respond to changes that had already occurred by steering change in a certain direction rather than allowing it to simply run its course. Solid biblical teaching, a new vision, and new people were all challenging the "old wineskins," and we were forced to either deal with a shifting world around us or fade away to insignificance. Even with a fresh vision in place, our systems and our church culture had to be examined, poked, prodded—and then examined again. We not only had to ask ourselves if we knew why we were doing what we were doing, but also if what we were doing was what really needed to be done, given the needs we faced.

Authentic change will affect everything in a church, just as it does in a person. The idea that "just one little thing" can be changed and the rest will all stay the same may sound good in a brainstorming session, but it will invariably cause unexpected systemic changes throughout an organism if it is implemented in the wrong way. And make no mistake, the biblical imagery of the church as the body of Christ supports the idea that those who are "in Christ" form an *organism*, not just an organization.

One of the continual delights in my life over the past decade has been to witness firsthand the incredible variety of body types the Lord Jesus chooses to form in this world. While churches share many important parts in common, they are strikingly unique in so many ways. Naturally, because my background gives me a common language and experience, I am astonished over the variety of Presbyterian cultures I encounter. But I am also overwhelmed by the unmistakable "life in Christ" that I find in so many other church cultures where people are striving to obey and respond to the One who has brought them into existence. It reminds me so vividly of the early years of our own transformation at the Brentwood church.

An atmosphere of responsiveness to God gradually brought our church to a place in the 1980s where we were willing to lay all we were and all we had before God and seek his guidance for our present and future. We set system changes in motion. We continued to uncover and analyze the underlying culture. We knew it needed to change. Certain parts needed to be recognized in new ways, other parts needed to be encouraged, while still others needed to be gracefully retired.

I can't emphasize enough how pointless it is to change a system and not address its underlying culture. The converse is true as well: You simply can't make changes in the culture without attending to the systems it drives. Admittedly, a system within a church can exist quite independently from the surrounding community. Your church is probably organized to function in ways that are different from any other organization in the community—except for other churches, of course. But the culture in your church does have strong links to the existing surrounding culture. To use an obvious example, a Baptist, Methodist, Lutheran, or Presbyterian church may be planted in either a big city or a rural town and still be clearly identifiable as a church from one of those denominations. But the ones located in cities will share points in common with each other that are quite distinct from their cousin rural churches. Many of these distinctions result from the effects of the surrounding culture.

The point I want to emphasize is that neither systemic nor cultural change can occur apart from each other. Mess with a culture, and the system will grind to a halt; alter a system, and the culture will react. I believe this is true because people instinctively understand that change can yield negative as well as positive results.

Sometimes people decide that if you can't predict the results, then maybe no change is better than even a little bit of change. The problem is that those who want to keep things exactly the way they've always been usually end up overwhelmed by the change that invariably takes place. Living into the church's biblical mandate is only possible through constant attention and adjustment to changes. What does this mean for the church? Once a church is functioning as a culture and a system that is alive for Christ, she will only remain so if she is continually open to change and adaptation—not simply inviting change for change's sake, but implementing biblically appropriate changes to stay engaged with what God is doing in the world.

CULTURE CHANGE

LIKE IT OR NOT, the current church culture in the United States still begins and ends with the senior pastor. Some of this is a carryover from past generations when the pastor was one of the best-educated persons in the community. He was expected to know at least a little about everything. Sometimes that assumption correctly appreciated the value of education. At other times, though, people assumed the pastor knew something about everything because God had told him!

In any case, deep-rooted cultural *change* in the church also begins with the pastor. Charles's faithful preaching and intentional actions began the general positive undermining of the existing culture. He gradually built into the church mind-set a new vocabulary of ministry that included "the people." We were starting to talk the talk of lay ministry long before we had begun to walk the walk of lay ministry. Although we didn't know it at the time, Charles was part of an important shift occurring in the way pastors themselves were thinking about ministry.

During the tumultuous years between 1960 and 1980, some remarkable changes came about in the way pastors functioned in our society. In the 60s the title "pastor" still meant someone who primarily preached the Word, taught the doctrines, and looked after "the flock." By the end of the 80s, the church growth movement had added the roles of "vision caster" and "chief executive officer" to the pastor's job description. These new subtitles meant that the pastor had be a preacher, a shepherd, and a professional leader. Soon a new emphasis was added to the pastor's to-do list—the role of "spiritual director." This continual expansion of responsibilities came with a curious oversight. Little or no attention was given to what the pastor ought *not* to do. All these roles, old and new together, were not evaluated with a view to determining what was essential for a pastor and what might be done by other people; the old roles were simply judged "not enough," and the burden of duties grew heavier and heavier.

Whatever the written job description of a pastor might be, the expectations almost always prove to be much broader. The job description remains part of the system, but what people *expect* a pastor's role to entail often has a lot more to do with the culture than the system—and rightly so. The system attempts to define the job in terms someone might think are doable. The culture expects the pastor to be all things to all people at all times. A written job description creates a somewhat artificial, yet measurable, accountability system for the pastor. But how can individual church members and the culture as a whole be held accountable for the dizzying variety of demands they sometimes make on the pastor?

As life has gotten more complex, pastors have been expected to know something about a lot more things. One of the healthiest decisions our pastor made was to acknowledge, particularly to himself first, that he *didn't* know everything. He worked, therefore, only from what he knew. He knew that the vision of an equipping church was right because it was biblical. He knew that if we kept working at honest, careful, and prayerful application of the Scriptures, we would make progress toward that vision. We needed that quiet confidence, as well as that cheerful ignorance, to carry us through the ups and downs of cultural change.

Whatever the written job description of a pastor, the expectations almost always prove to be much broader.

It has become painfully clear to me that the traditional view of the pastorate sets up both pastors and congregations for failure. This fact became real to us at Brentwood as we stumbled over the veiled expectations we had about our pastor. We kept finding things he couldn't do. Not only could he not leap over buildings in a single bound (even if the elders asked him nicely), he found it impossible to be in two places at the same time. Sometimes it was downright shocking how little our pastor knew about certain areas of life. Almost everyone in our church who had expertise in some area found that they knew a lot more than our pastor about that particular area. Now in the traditional picture, this would have been cause for dismay and disappointment. But we began to realize that the pastor wasn't supposed to know and do everything. The fact that some of us knew more about certain things didn't mean he was shirking his responsibilities or betraying his lack of perfection—it simply meant that we had stumbled on an area in which he genuinely needed our help!

My partner in ministry, Brad Smith, likes to tell the story of a pastor who found himself too tired to be dishonest. In the middle of a meeting with the trustees, as they discussed what to do about a crowded facility, he decided he didn't know the answer to this genuine problem. The congregation was supportive of the option of replacing the building. The next step needed to be made. The trustees looked at the pastor. He looked back at them. He finally sighed deeply and said, "I don't really know what to do about this. We've prayed. I'm going home." He got up and left. The trustees looked at each other, and it finally dawned on them that sitting there among them were a real-estate broker, an investment banker, and an advertising executive. They had more practical expertise in this area than the pastor could have ever dreamed about possessing. Working together they came up with an effective solution to the church facility problem. The pastor's wisest move had been to get out of their way.

It seems so obvious now, but we really struggled to put into action the discovery that our pastor wasn't supposed to know and do everything. As long as our culture operated under the assumption that the pastor *could* do everything, the corollary was that we could do nothing. If, however, the Bible passages that describe the church as an organism speak the truth, then the idea of the all-purpose, all-sufficient, all-knowing, all-doing pastor must be wrong. We knew there had to be a healthier, more biblical way to do ministry than the way our culture was dictating.

Of course, it is true that some duties are uniquely the pastor's responsibility. In addition to preaching, teaching, casting the vision, and modeling shared ministry, the pastor must be an advocate for the vision. As you follow the story of our experience at Brentwood, you will see this truth illustrated over and over. Without Charles's support and advocacy, particularly when I wasn't sure what I was doing, all the other pieces of the puzzle would have never come together.

MEGACHURCH OPTIONS

EVEN AS WE LABORED to reshape our Brentwood church culture into one that more nearly mirrored the biblical picture, an astonishing development was occurring in the wider Christian culture. I watched with amazement the rise of the megachurch in America.

I'm still not sure I completely understand God's purposes in allowing such localized superpowered churches to succeed, but I find myself wanting to learn as much as I can from what they are doing right. I have spent enough time in and around megachurches to know that most of the criticisms leveled against them flow out of jealousy and frustration.

Names like Bill Hybels and Rick Warren represent heroes to some, but just "too popular to be up to any good" leaders to others. Your own denomination probably has a few names of pastors and churches that instantly create discussion. Both men mentioned above, and others, have written extensively about their philosophy of ministry and the development of the churches they lead. They have functioned within systems that can be reproduced elsewhere. Both Willow Creek Community Church and Saddleback Valley Community Church incorporate many of the principles of lay ministry we discuss in this book. I have watched these principles function in people's lives in these churches.

For example, in a visit to Willow Creek I had a few moments of conversation with the person who gave my group a tour of the facilities. He was so knowledgeable about the church that I assumed he was a paid staff member. In response to my question about his primary role in the church, he used a phrase I'll never forget. He said, "I get to pursue my passion for the graphic arts by helping with the development of various printed materials for the church." He said it with the kind of enthusiasm that underlined his expressive words. Someone had intentionally recognized (or maybe stumbled on) his gifts and passion and invited him to participate. He was having so much fun that the idea of getting paid hadn't occurred to him. Not because his work wasn't worth something (he was making an excellent salary in the business world with his talent), but because the value of his talent made it a significant gift to present to the Lord.

It seems to me, however, that there are two drawbacks to keep in mind when considering whether to incorporate the Willow Creek or the Saddleback model into a particular local church. The first of these is that both these churches were started from scratch. Their cultures and systems developed side by side in a relatively short time span. They have honored and incorporated obedience to biblical principles, but they had few pieces of denominational, cultural, or historical luggage to carry with them. The freedom to adapt and change has been kept close to the core of their systems, so that they are able to make adjustments to respond to the needs they discover along the way.

This freedom to change is based on the passion both Bill and Rick have for reaching the unchurched. Neither is particularly interested in providing another entertaining alternative for bored Christians who are shopping for the latest and greatest. Both these pastors and the teams they've invited to join them have targeted a part of the American culture populated by the unchurched. They are driven to reach these people with the gospel.

The second drawback to adopting the megachurch model is that, while you may incorporate similar structures to the ones in their churches, you will never be either Bill Hybels or Rick Warren. God has uniquely gifted these men for the role they are performing in the body of Christ. You may do well to observe and imitate them, but you cannot be them.

One of the great lessons we can learn from these men is their ability to see the culture around them. Rick Warren, in his book *The Purpose-Driven Church*, has a wonderful chapter on church culture called "What Drives Your Church?" While he doesn't use *culture* as the defining word, culture is what he's talking about. He writes the following:

> Every church is driven by something. There is a guiding force, a controlling assumption, a directing conviction behind everything that happens. It may be unspoken. It may be unknown to many. Most likely it's never been officially voted on. But it is there, influencing every aspect of the church's life.[1]

In the rest of the chapter that follows this comment, Rick offers a number of suggestions that deserve the attention of any church seeking to understand her present culture.

One of the great lessons we can learn from both these men is their ability to see the culture around them.

The results of the congregational self-examination I experienced with Brentwood Presbyterian closely resemble the kind of observations Rick makes. The purpose-driven church and the equipping church do not compete with each other. The terms simply describe a different part of the biblical picture. "Purpose" describes how a church sees herself as a whole; "equipping" describes how a church sees the relationship between the whole and her members.

Meanwhile, the megachurch has become part of the American church cultural landscape. Though the idea has been interpreted as a surefire package in some churches, it has often failed because it tends to challenge the prevailing culture in too many places without recognizing the need to preserve much of that culture. It also tends to be the sole property of the senior pastor.

When the pastor's vision for the church's system, culture, and programming has been borrowed lock, stock, and barrel from someone else,

---

[1]Rick Warren, *The Purpose-Driven® Church* (Grand Rapids: Zondervan, 1995), 77.

it has a hard time taking root in a group. In such cases pastors tend to operate as CEOs or corporate business leaders. They are so busy running the system and program that there is little or no time left to actually pastor. I'm meeting more and more pastors who report that their work has been joyless. Their own sense of purpose has been undermined because they don't have the skills to do all that the new system requires of them. When pastors adopt someone else's ministry as a package, they don't give themselves or their churches a fair shot at growing into a new way of doing things. When I meet these men and women of God, they are often burned-out and discouraged because they've realized they were pursuing goals quite distant from Scripture's teachings.

Like the Willow Creek and Saddleback churches, Brentwood has experienced significant growth in the past decade. Based on membership statistics alone, we are also in the top 3 percent of all Protestant churches in the nation. None of these churches set out to be big; they set out to be obedient. They were planted, or they undertook changes, with both the Bible and culture in mind. They all represent an interesting application of Paul's comment about division of labor in ministry: "I planted the seed, Apollos watered it, but God made it grow. So neither he who plants nor he who waters is anything, but only God, who makes things grow" (1 Corinthians 3:6–7).

The leaders of these churches would be the first to say that their remarkable size has given them an audience and a platform to share principles and values, but that their core principles are true in small churches as well. In fact, a careful look at the life of a megachurch will usually quickly reveal a major emphasis on connecting people in a way that makes them feel part of something small and intimate (as well as feeling a part of something large).

BACK HOME

I AM ACUTELY AWARE that you read these words from within a certain cultural context. Whether you are a new pastor or an established one, or whether you are a leader within your church who takes seriously your role and gives direction to others, remember that you are part of a history. If you are planting a new church, God has already been in the field ahead of you. Discerning and following God's guidance will depend on how well you can determine where you are right now. How clearly can you define and describe the culture in which you minister?

Time spent mapping and understanding the culture of your church and community will not be wasted. What we discovered at Brentwood shaped our direction and provided some of the keys to success.

Know Your Culture

I meet pastors all the time who are trapped in a fortress mentality. They want to create a kingdom inside their church walls that people will inhabit. They somehow assume that the movie cliché "If you build it, they will come" applies to the church. The reverse is closer to the truth: "If you build them, it will come."

When I suggest to pastors that they walk around the community that surrounds their church building, they often react as if this were a new idea. I'm not pushing door-to-door evangelism as a technique here. I'm just suggesting having some kind of face-to-face contact with each of the homes a block or two in every direction from the church. You may find that opportunities for evangelism will come. Start by finding out enough to know whether these families need to be evangelized. If you have already done so, I commend this enthusiastically!

You also need to immerse yourself in the history of your church. Who can tell you why things are the way they are? If there is no written or photographic history of the church, encourage the people to start compiling one. You will learn a lot if you can get people to talk about the past. The stories everyone knows should become familiar to you as well, for in these stories you will find insights about the culture of your church and community.

Some Things Shouldn't Change

When we acknowledge and appreciate what shouldn't be changed in our churches, we create a trusting atmosphere. When the discussion about change gives the impression that nothing is sacred, resistance will often be fierce. If our own assumption is that everything must be changed, then we probably haven't looked closely enough at what God has already done.

God Is at Work Everywhere

I find it all too easy to develop an Elijah syndrome: "I alone am still faithful to you, Lord!" Churches that define themselves as the sole representatives of God in a community run the risk of offending God by reducing him to their small image. Even within a church, the healthiest changes come when, as a starting point, people take time to ask what God is already doing rather than assuming that God is doing nothing.

Culture and System Interact

As you try to implement in your situation the lessons from chapters 3 and 4, you may find it hard to distinguish clearly between culture and system. The "who we are" of culture and the "what we do" of system do mix at times. Better to list the same characteristic in both categories than to struggle to have two entirely distinct lists. Certain obvious questions will generate many insights: How does culture define the role of our pastor in comparison with how the system expects the pastor to function? If a crisis arises, how do both system and culture inform our response as a church?

Open the Process to Team Study

Every step of the transformational process ought to be open to as many people as possible. Invite people to help you look at the church. Identify people who have the propensity to analyze and offer them the opportunity to put their skills to good use in developing a picture of the culture and systems of your church. Specific tasks like this will give you great insight later on in knowing which people to invite to join other teams within the church.

The various teams that formed in Brentwood during the early years of our transformation were amazing. I think of them primarily as uniquely gifted people drawn together to accomplish what I couldn't even dream of! The effectiveness and ministry of the computer team, the creative worship team, my own lay ministry team, and many others still warm my heart every time I think of them. I know what Paul meant when he told his friends in Philippi, "I thank my God every time I remember you" (Philippians 1:3).

Evaluate Pastoral Expectations—and Everyone Else's Too

Behind many departures from pastoral ministry we discover an uncomfortable truth of ill-defined and continuously expanding expectations. Paul's rhetorical expression about being all things to all people sometimes gets applied as the exact job description for the pastor. More than one pastor has expressed growing despair over trying to succeed in a situation where every church member seems to insist on having his or her own set of accountability factors to which the pastor must submit. The fact is, even where pastoral responsibilities are spelled out in writing, there are frequently situations where other church leaders must declare that the pastor will not be held to the "shadow job descriptions" that individuals develop along the way.

It is helpful from time to time to review everyone's responsibilities within the body. One way to develop an antidote to the tendency to expand the pastor's responsibilities is to develop a list of specific functions the pastor is *not* expected to do. What should naturally follow is discussion regarding the importance of these nonpastoral functions. If we don't expect the pastor to be responsible for these things, who will see to it that they get done? It is also helpful to look at the pastor's stated job description with the following helpful question in mind: To what degree does each of these duties contribute to the pastor's biblical duty of equipping the saints?

Make Sure to Leave Room for Connection

One of the principles of effective megachurches is the admission that their health depends on the number of "microchurches" they harbor. Ministry teams within megachurches accomplish some of the key biblical principles of fellowship and connection that cannot be accomplished in the large setting of a particular church at worship. These and other small groups provide the personal touch and accountability required for healthy connection in the body of Christ.

What does this mean? Biblical faithfulness and genuine life in the body of Christ has little to do with how many more than two or three are gathered in Christ's name. What they are doing together matters more for eternity than how many are doing it!

EQUIPPING HEROES

Calvary Church
St. Louis, Missouri
www.CalvaryMidRivers.org
Senior Pastor: Dave Michelson

"People Development" is the name of the ministry launched at Calvary Church in St. Louis, Missouri. The church had a desire not just to be an equipping church, but a caring church as well. So the focus had two directions—discovery and facilitating care. This was to become their identity, their DNA, their culture.

Their senior pastor, Dave Michelson, states, "The senior pastor has to breathe it, walk it, live it, teach it, not just one time but day in and day out." In the early stages the leadership team took seriously the need to find the right person who desired to be a part of a team that placed a high value on systems skills and on caring. To instill the values for the culture was and is the responsibility of the leadership, and staff alignment was critical to its success. It started with both board and staff. They realized that they needed to share the same value system that says, "I am the equipper, not the doer." If not, there were going to be immense roadblocks to effectively mobilizing people for ministry.

What cannot be understated is the amount of time and patience it takes to change a culture. At Calvary it took two-and-a-half sometimes painful years of working through staffing issues and establishing values. In some cases the process involved undoing some assumptions from a mind-set that the pastor was the key to the church. Dave observes that it can be extremely painful for staff to realize that "Christ is the key; the people are the army, and we are just the captains." Not every team member could make that transition in thinking and some chose to leave rather than shift styles. Working with the staff to address culture issues was the key. They organized a number of retreats on the difference between doers and leaders; they took advantage of outside training opportunities; they studied Scriptures and got reeducated in a biblical and a practical mind-set.

To keep growing into equipping leaders they used an intentional goal-setting process driven by the senior pastor, the gatekeeper or protector of the DNA. They redefined what success would look like. Dave shared an example. "My pastors used to say, 'That group I led went just great, and they feel good about it.' Now they say to me, 'The guy I got leading that group just did the greatest job I have ever seen.' And that is a radical redefinition of success."

Without the senior pastor working from the top down to create alignment within the staff and governing boards, it is virtually impossible to change the culture.

QUESTIONS FOR REFLECTION AND DISCUSSION

1. How do your current systems reflect your culture and serve your people?

2. What areas of your ministry lack effective systems to support both laypeople and leadership? What are the first steps to building new ones?

3. What is the guiding force or controlling assumption that drives your church?

4. What would your staff say if asked to define the culture of your church?

5. What would others—both members and those outside the walls of your church—say about your church culture?

5

Checking the Conveyer Belts at the Exits

And He Himself gave some to be apostles, some prophets, some evangelists, and some pastors and teachers, for the equipping of the saints for the work of ministry, for the edifying of the body of Christ, *till* we all come to the unity of the faith and the knowledge of the Son of God, to a perfect man, to the measure of the stature of the fullness of Christ.

Ephesians 4:11–13 NKJV, emphasis added

IN THE PHRASE "till we all come to the unity of the faith," I find "till" to be an interesting word. I appreciate it in this translation of Ephesians 4:13 because it stops me for a moment. Though an obvious conjunction of until, the unexpected form of the word causes me to repeat the sound several times as I think about its significance.

The word *till* refers to a time frame. In this case, God gave certain kinds of people for certain kinds of roles to be carried out till certain objectives have been reached. If those objectives have not yet been reached, then the roles are still required.

Not only are the roles still required, but so are those with whom the roles are to be carried out. In other words, the saints have to stick around long enough for the apostles, prophets, evangelists, pastors, and teachers to do their work. If any group is missing, progress toward God's objectives will be delayed.

When members and leaders within Christ's church drift from local church to local church without commitment, long-term spiritual health for individuals, as well as churches, suffers notable setbacks. Churches that are serious about genuine growth pay attention to how people arrive and how they leave the church.

ORGANISMS RARELY SURVIVE as disconnected miscellaneous parts. Bodies don't function efficiently with breakaway members. The concept of membership includes the idea of permanence. As we began to take seriously the role of every member at Brentwood, we quickly discovered that our membership was a continuously changing group. We knew some of the reasons:

- Our church was located in an unusually mobile part of the country, and members moved away regularly.
- Our church body represented the cycle of life, with potential new members being born into families while long-standing members died.
- We had visiting families and individuals almost every week, but many did not return.
- From time to time people simply left the congregation for a variety of reasons.

When we analyzed our findings, we arrived at several conclusions:

- Mobility was rapidly becoming a fact of life in our society, and it was a reality largely outside of our control.
- Life goes on, and when a member of a local church dies, those who remain on earth take comfort in the fact that Christ's church is the only organization that never loses a member because of death.
- We were already seeing an improvement in retaining visitors because, as part of our tracking procedures, we were intentionally showing genuine interest in the new people who came through our doors. We accepted the fact that not every person who visited would eventually find their church home with us, but we decided we had to continually monitor and improve our ways of welcoming and caring for new people.
- When we came to the issue of people leaving, a creeping sense of unease seemed to enter the discussion. We thought we had a pretty good handle on why some people were leaving—they sensed change in the air and protested by their absence. Others were spiritually dissatisfied or offended in some way, so they left. These departures demanded our attention. We wanted to make sure we weren't losing members for the wrong reasons.

ASSIMILATION

WE QUICKLY DISCOVERED that we were among many churches trying to slow down the "revolving door" and close the "back door." The theory was that if a church could simply develop the right kind of welcome for people, more of them would stay. I began to hear of churches hiring pastors of assimilation who were responsible to make sure people felt welcome and "plugged in."

Churches that accepted the idea that an aggressive and intentional welcome might be an effective way to get visitors to return developed some elaborate ways to carry out this plan. My partner at Leadership Training Network, Brad Smith, tells about visiting a church in which they encountered firsthand one of these "full-court press" assimilation plans. Their experience on Sunday morning was pleasant. They were recognized as visitors and asked for some basic information. Over lunch, Brad and his wife discussed their morning. Their first impression of the church had generally been positive. The preaching had been good, the worship was enthusiastic, the programs of the church seemed nicely balanced, and the people were friendly.

When they arrived home after lunch, they found a welcome gift from the church—a plant placed by their front door. Later, a woman from the church stopped by because she noticed their car in the driveway. (Brad made a mental note to begin storing his car in the garage.) She invited them to attend the Sunday evening service, at which, by the way, she was singing. Monday evening brought a small group of visitors from the church. On Tuesday an official letter of welcome arrived from the church. Wednesday evening included a visit from the pastor. All of these contacts were unannounced. Though it was surely not the church's intention, Brad and his wife felt like targets. They were overwelcomed, and they decided not to return to that church.

> **One couple described the effects as being "dated hard, married quick, and then ignored."**

Giving attention to the way a church welcomes people can be a valuable part of fostering healthy growth. But getting people in the door "for keeps" takes a lot more than a slick, or even genuine, welcome mat. Brad reports that he's had a number of conversations with people who have joined churches with elaborate programs of assimilation, and these folks frequently expressed disappointment. The intense, warm, and persistent efforts to get people to return and stay at the church were typically not followed up with a church life that showed the same kind of warm interest and enthusiasm. One couple described the effects as being "dated hard, married quick, and then ignored."

QUIET DEPARTURES

MANY PEOPLE WHOSE EXPERIENCE is that of being "dated hard . . . and then ignored" rarely make a fuss when they leave a church. But they often leave disappointed, disillusioned, and even angry. Their feelings are often tragically confirmed by the fact that their absence may even go unnoticed. They got into church all right, but the church never got into them; they were let in easily enough, but they never belonged. They found themselves numbered, but they never felt they were counted on. In sad cases like these, says Brad, "The church hasn't closed the back door; it has simply lengthened the hallway."

When I attended church growth seminars in the mid-1980s, I heard a lot about assimilation. I knew it was an area we would have to address. In my simple way of thinking I realized that *every* active layperson, including myself, had at one time been a visitor and a stranger. I kept my ears open for ways we could improve our efforts to help people move from warming the pews to participating in the flames of church life.

During one of these seminars hosted by Church Growth Institute, one of the presenters made an offhand (and certainly unexpected) comment in which he noted that the largest percentage of members leaving churches were former elders and deacons. I was stunned. Why was I worrying about keeping visitors coming back so they would eventually join the church if those who had invested so much in the church were leaving?

At the time, we were still wrestling with the idea of tracking our people, so I really had no basis for either refuting or agreeing with the presenter's conclusions. But I knew I needed to find out if Brentwood fit that model. I asked Charles the following week if he knew what percentage of our membership losses were coming from among the leadership of the church. He didn't know, but he was also eager to find out.

In the Presbyterian tradition people are ordained as elders and deacons for life. They are recognized as leaders within the church, and with that recognition goes the assumption that the character and qualities that make someone a leader do not leave a person once he or she has reached that level of spiritual maturity. Their roles and responsibilities may vary within the church over time, but the tradition understands the ongoing value of these experienced believers. The church governing structure itself insists on a rotation of leadership in order to allow for personal renewal and for new leadership. Rotation of leadership also guards against burnout.

When Charles and I checked the records, we discovered more absentee elders and deacons than we expected. We counted eighteen leaders who seemed inactive. They hadn't moved away, but they were missing. I had been in the church now for years, and some of these names were unfamiliar to me. We knew we needed some fact-finding and rapid intervention. We decided to get these leaders together and informally discuss with them their experience as former leaders. Today we would have called this a "mass exit interview." Back then we were scrambling to find out what we were doing wrong and shamelessly trying to make corrections along the way.

My husband, an elder who was not on session at the time, and I hosted a dessert in our home. Charles and I sent invitations to all eighteen former leaders. We both signed the letter of invitation that stated the purpose of the gathering. To our delight, sixteen people responded positively. (I met a couple of them for the first time that evening!) We hadn't planned an elaborate program; we simply had a lot of questions, most of which didn't get asked. When the group realized that we really wanted their input, the floodgates of information, feelings, observations, corrections, and revelation opened. We let them know we wanted the truth—both positive and negative comments on their terms of service in the church. How could the church have helped improve their experience before, during, and after they served in significant roles? They literally took over the discussion.

I sat there taking it all in and marveling over the untapped decades of rich church experience that filled my living room that evening. Partly because they vastly outnumbered us, and partly because of their love for Christ's church, they shared a lot of wisdom and insight with us during those hours.

Most of them felt in some significant way unappreciated for their service. The fact that the church's lack of gratitude was unintended didn't remove the hurts. Some felt that their rotation out of office had been a dismissal from service. To them it felt like they had been removed rather than reassigned. Those who had been encouraged to take a "rest" from leadership had sometimes felt this was a code for rejection. The truth was, some of them didn't feel tired. Their courageous effort of service and strong commitment to the church had not been recognized or valued beyond what felt like a generic formality, and they were hurt.

A few leaders reported that they felt poorly trained for most of the functions they had been asked to carry out. They recalled too many times when they had to figure things out on their own. And then, just about the time they had finally gotten to the point of some confidence, they were relieved of the duty. Rarely had they been asked to train their replacements. In fact, they felt their hard-earned experience most often simply went ignored.

We concluded some important things that night. We had a lot to learn about training, assigning, keeping, reassigning, and affirming our leaders. What's more, we needed to do something immediately to recognize the large pool of leaders who were part of our local church. This decision led to the formation of what became known as the "Fellowship of the Ordained" at Brentwood Presbyterian Church.

THE FELLOWSHIP OF THE ORDAINED

THE BIBLICAL MODEL of leadership includes the requirement of service. Jesus shared these stunning words with his disciples:

> You know that in this world kings are tyrants, and officials lord it over the people beneath them. But among you it should be quite different. Whoever wants to be a leader among you must be your servant, and whoever wants to be first must be the slave of all. For even I, the Son of Man, came here not to be served but to serve others, and to give my life as a ransom for many.
>
> Mark 10:42–45 NLT

I have often pondered what Jesus meant by his last statement. I understand and accept the fact that he gave his life as a ransom for me, the ultimate act of service. What I have wondered about is the "not to be served" phrase. For when I read the Gospels, I find that Jesus did allow others to serve him quite frequently. And he affirmed their service.

One of my favorite examples is the account of Jesus' visit to the home of Simon (see Luke 7:36–50). During that meal, a disreputable woman came and knelt behind Jesus, weeping all over his feet, wiping them with her hair, and pouring costly perfume on them. In response to Simon's critical thoughts Jesus told a devastating parable and drew this conclusion:

> Look at this woman kneeling here. When I entered your home, you didn't offer me water to wash the dust from my feet, but she has washed them with her tears and wiped them with her hair. You didn't give me a kiss of greeting, but she has kissed my feet again and again from the time I first came in. You neglected the courtesy of olive oil to anoint my head, but she has anointed my feet with rare perfume. I tell you, her sins—and they are many—have been forgiven, so she has shown me much love. But a person who is forgiven little shows only little love.
>
> Luke 7:44–47 NLT

Jesus didn't define leadership as a position in which a person rejects the service of others. His primary concern was to caution his followers about seeking leadership positions in order to receive the service of others.

My own experience among church leaders has repeatedly confirmed Jesus' observations. The leaders most difficult to work with in church settings usually fall into one of two categories: those who refuse to recognize, appreciate, or ask for the service of others, even when they clearly need it, and those who assume that because they fill a leadership role others ought to serve them. Graciousness in serving and being served marks the lives of leaders who have made the largest impact on my life. I can't help but note that, even though the reasons were deeply saddening, the joy my husband and I experienced in being able to serve our pastor, Charles, during his illness was immeasurable.

Thus, it was a natural outcome of our gathering with the first sixteen "retired" leaders to announce the inaugural dinner of the Fellowship of the Ordained. From the outset, we structured the time to honor the value we placed on peer relationships and accountability. We extended the invitation to a mailing list of one hundred former elders and deacons who had been ordained in our church or who had come from other churches to membership at Brentwood. Of these, seventy-five attended the first gathering.

Graciousness in serving and being served marks the lives of leaders who have made the largest impact on my life.

The combined experience and wisdom of our church members once again impressed me. Many of them had been individually recognized for special service and contributions over the years, but this was the first time their role as a leadership group in the church received public affirmation. That night we began to rely on this group as a significant component in the decision-making processes of our church. At any one time, many of them are filling active roles within the structure of the church. But together they supply a corporate wisdom we now know we can't afford to overlook.

In subsequent years the Fellowship of the Ordained has continued to function in many effective ways. They are kept informed about the ongoing work and current thinking of the church's leaders. They are often invited to give counsel in specific matters where their expertise is valued. When they are invited to serve in specific active roles, they are better prepared to serve because they know what's going on in the church at large.

One noticeable but quite unexpected by-product of recognizing and affirming our leaders has been the overall health and encouragement that has spread across the entire church. Affirmed leadership tends to filter the effects throughout the whole body. Valued leaders find new ways to serve others effectively. And those growing toward leadership positions are encouraged to know that their efforts will be appreciated.

As of this writing we recently celebrated the fourteenth annual dinner of the Fellowship of the Ordained. The group has an identity. They know they are a valued sounding board for the whole body. They know the pastoral staff and the current lay leaders of the church appreciate them and rely on them as a leadership grid to ensure that the church is moving forward with wisdom, biblical clarity, and broad-based support.

What began as an intentional and somewhat artificial attempt to correct past errors has become a key component of our church life. It remains an intentional part of our structure because we now understand the value of such a group. It remains intentional because we want everything we do as a church to be intentional; we want all our actions and structures to have clear reasons and purposes for existence. The Fellowship of the Ordained offers us a further opportunity to practice and model the kind of love and caring that ought to characterize a local church. Genuine caring always includes both opportunities to serve and to be served.

THE BACK DOOR

THE BACK DOOR OF the church can't be locked. People can, and will, leave. Their departures will happen for many reasons—some of them good. Let's not let their leaving go unnoticed. If they leave as an act of rebuke, let's make sure we have listened. If they are right, we may have to apologize, and we may have an opportunity to correct the mistake so others don't leave for the same reason. If they are wrong, we are commanded to forgive; they may eventually come back, and we may have an . opportunity to serve with them again. If they leave as a result of relocation, we need to celebrate their contributions to the body and corporately pray for them as they seek a new church family.

If the back door can't be locked, what then can we do about it? We can make sure we haven't inadvertently installed a conveyor belt of inattentiveness that carries people out of the church. We can make sure we serve people while they are among us and deeply appreciate their service to us. People often try the back door because they've come to think they won't be missed if they leave. People who are affirmed for what they do and are effectively served by others in the church usually forget where the back door is located.

EQUIPPING PRINCIPLES

Notice Who's Leaving . . . and Why

Departures communicate. The way in which people stop doing what they were doing, or the way they respond to change, says a lot about their experience and their feelings. Absences in church often shout for attention—not always, but often enough that a genuinely caring church that desires to equip her members for service to Christ will want to know (and will figure out a way to find out) why people have drifted away.

It takes much less time to guess what a person might be feeling than to skillfully draw those thoughts and feelings into the open. We would often rather jump to conclusions about others because discovering the truth may be painful or uncomfortable. When we find out the reasons a person is leaving or has created "distance," we may have to correct an error, rethink a position, stand firm in some way, or make an apology. All of this takes time and emotional energy.

A person who has really been heard may still not decide to stay or even to reengage immediately. Sometimes people do need to leave. There are good, honest, and necessary reasons for departures. The point of integrity for the church doesn't have so much to do with the question "Can we hold on to everyone who walks through our door?" as with the question "Have we been faithful to Christ in the way we have treated each person who walks through our door?"

Make Time for Affirmation and Appreciation

Systems and structures offer methods for remembering what needs to be done, but they seldom accomplish their ultimate purposes without personal attention and participation. We can establish traditions such as "Teacher Appreciation Sunday," "Leadership Recognition Dinner," or "The Towel and Basin Awards" as specific settings in which to express gratitude for service. These have the potential for creating a powerful sense of belonging and affirmation for people, but they will fail if they come across as thoughtless and automatic. People know what is genuine, and what is not.

Discovering, listing, and publishing people's significant events, such as birthdays and anniversaries, can be beneficial, but the effort becomes hollow if it is purely mechanical. The effort to personalize affirmation and appreciation takes time!

Learn That Duties May Cease, but Roles Usually Don't

The church doesn't hand out spiritual gifts, personal talents, and special character traits; these are evidence of God's grace. The church can help identify these powerful tools and provide opportunities for their use. Because the gifts have been given for the benefit of others, an equipping church attends to all the ways in which believers can exercise and keep growing in their various gifts.

One of the most valuable lessons I learned through the Fellowship of the Ordained came when I realized that a person does not retire from their spiritual gifts or areas of godly leadership. Mature believers are a priceless treasure in the church. Until they are transferred to service in God's heavenly kingdom, they have a role in the earthly outpost called the church. Duties in that outpost may change from time to time. Rest and reflection also make up part of the cycle of active participation in the body of Christ, but only God decides when our tour of duty is over. We have been designed and called to offer a unique contribution to others, and as long as we remain on this side of heaven, God has work to do in us and through us.

Conduct Exit Interviews

We still use the term *exit interview* at Brentwood to describe the way we want to handle changes in service opportunities. These are not really our conversations with people who are leaving the church. The *exit* part merely accents the leaving of one area of service in order to take up another responsibility or to enjoy a time of refreshment; the *interview* part attempts to convey that we as a church body do not want to make assumptions regarding the person's past experience or future desires. We want to know, so we ask.

Two primary values are expressed and accomplished by the interview: (1) affirming their gift of time and service to the church and (2) listening well for what was successful and where there were challenges that we as church leaders can learn from and improve on.

Pastoral staff members never participate in exit interviews. What the church needs to know can best be discovered through interactions between peers. Therefore, the only people invited to do exit interviews at Brentwood are members of the Fellowship of the Ordained. They do so with amazing grace and skill. We have come to understand that part of the information gained may be negative. There may be criticism of other leaders. Offenses may be aired. Constructive suggestions may be expressed that might be hard for some leaders to hear.

Because we value the truth and the wisdom we gain in exit interviews, we have made it clear that these are anonymous, but not confidential, conversations. What is said in these interviews will be discussed, while at the same time every effort will be made to guard the identity of the source from those who do not need to know. This helps us in several ways:

- It prevents the interview from becoming nothing more than a venting time in which the interviewer has been bound to silence and secrecy.
- It creates a situation in which the truth of the observations can be evaluated apart from the source.
- It takes some of the defensiveness out of handling criticisms.
- It fosters an atmosphere in which complaints and suggestions are treated seriously. The interview itself can be an important first step in a process of forgiveness and reconciliation. Often the offended party assumes that their point of pain is obvious to everyone else. When they find out that the pastor or another leader doesn't know that he or she has committed an offense, the possibility of correction presents itself.

Identify and Equip Individuals Who Have the Gift of Conversation

Each of us knows someone with a gift for conversation. They have a way of asking questions, stating opinions, and revealing themselves that draws other people out. They seem to know what you want or need to talk about. They often convey honor on a person by asking for his or her thoughts. They make it possible to discuss even difficult subjects within a nonthreatening atmosphere.

The quest for good "information gatherers" within a church often begins with the question, "Do we know someone whom everyone enjoys talking to?" Whether it is in conducting exit interviews, meeting with visitors, or helping with gift assessments, these skilled conversationalists can be a hidden strength in a congregation. Identifying them and equipping them so that their gifts are applied in ministry can have a powerful and widespread effect throughout a church.

Identify Teams, Again

As you can see from this chapter, the more I learned about the church, the more complex the picture became. During these past years I've grown in many ways, and so much of the growth has come through my team experiences. Almost every time I use "I" as I tell these stories, I'm actually referring to a small or large team that helped me and learned these lessons with me.

The complex organism called the church does not function in a healthy manner without multiple interdependent teams. These must be identified and assembled as the process of transformation proceeds. For instance, the valuable work of exit interviews could not have been carried forward without a wonderful team who did what the pastor could not have done. The subject of exit interviews often involved disappointments or disagreements about the direction of ministry. We found that people were more honest with a fellow layperson. To their credit our pastoral staff surely wanted to know if unintentional offense had been caused or if there were blind spots that needed correction. The effectiveness of this team can be seen in the fact that the exit interviews sometimes turned into recommitment interviews with members who finally felt they were being heard by someone.

Invest the Gift of Time

Almost every principle in this chapter requires a central ingredient, namely, *time*. (The same could be said about the whole book.) A church does not equip without investing enormous amounts of time. The idea of "fast equipping" offers an empty temptation. What is a central organic function within the body of Christ becomes just another instant answer in an age of instant solutions that ultimately don't work.

I spent my first eighteen months as a director of lay ministries just beginning to understand many of these principles. That was only the first installment of time. Years of time investment followed. But all along there were others who invested untold thousands of hours in the life of our church. As much as we have learned about expressing appreciation, only Christ will convey the ultimate affirmation in the words "Well done, good and faithful servant!" (Matthew 25:21).

I began this chapter with some thoughts about the word *till*. Those whom God has gifted as apostles, prophets, evangelists, pastors, and teachers have been called to use their time in certain ways. They are definitely not called to do everything. There are certain crucial ministries and opportunities to which they will undoubtedly have to say no.

The Bible offers insight into how leaders can effectively refuse ministry that exceeds the bounds of their specific calling. One example comes from Acts 6:1–7. Up to this point, the church had been functioning with her original leadership team, Jesus' apostles. But growth in numbers and changing needs were creating a leadership vacuum. The problem showed up in the form of complaints. In response, the apostles demonstrated leadership by finding more leaders. Note what the Twelve said: "We apostles should spend our time preaching and teaching the word of God, not administering a food program" (Acts 6:2 NLT). They didn't say the food program shouldn't or couldn't be done because they didn't have time; they simply affirmed their own call and urged the church to identify another leadership team to meet this need for ministry. The results were continued growth because more people were participating in Christ's work.

An equipping church understands that believers make the best investment of their time when they are operating in the area of their call from God. This has little to do with busyness and much to do with effectiveness. An equipping church measures success by the number of members who understand God's call in their lives and are finding ways to live out that call inside the church and out in the world.

EQUIPPING HEROES

Oak Hills Church of Christ
San Antonio, Texas
www.oakhillschurchofchrist.org
Senior Pastor: Max Lucado
Minister of Membership: Pat Hile

Oak Hills Church of Christ has learned through trial and error the ideas and programs that work best for their culture. The Church of Christ is, by her history and design, a lay-driven church. Committed to honoring and valuing her leadership, Oak Hills' first "launch" has been one of appreciation for those who currently serve as leaders in the church. The goal is to value and assess the strengths and needs of Oak Hills through the very leaders who are running the ministries. They have developed a special team with just the right skill and enthusiasm to carry out this assessment under a clear and memorable set of guidelines:

ANTS Team = A Need To Serve.
We are the ANTS Team because:
- We work underground, behind the scenes.
- We work as a team.
- We are persistent and hardworking. We don't give up.
- Our specialty is overcoming obstacles.
- We serve a King, not a queen.

The ANTS team serves as evaluators and assessors of the global vision for effective equipping ministry. The team was commissioned by the elders to develop a churchwide process to help members and newcomers (1) discover their gifts, (2) acknowledge their needs, and (3) find a place of service so they can mature in Christ. Part of this process involves finding out what is happening at Oak Hills. The ANTS developed a survey designed to uncover the many wonderful activities, projects, processes, and events already happening in their church family.

The ANTS survey focuses on the seven components of a churchwide involvement process:

- Assimilation
- Bible Context
- Discovery
- Matching
- Placement
- Coaching
- Recognition

These components are all to be supported with an effective and strong administrative system.

In concert with their senior pastor, Max Lucado, the ANTS team hosted a dinner for all ministry leaders. At the dinner the pastor cast the biblical vision for the equipping church. The team then affirmed the existing leadership of the church and introduced the need to assess the current situation—where the strengths were and where they needed to provide additional support to various ministries. Subsequently, through a trained team of interviewers, the team began an ongoing survey of all ministry leaders presently in service to determine where they were in relation to the seven components and where they needed support.

The wisdom in their process exhibits these important values: (1) including and valuing *all* ministry leaders, (2) senior pastor advocacy for the biblical model they are seeking to implement, (3) affirming the strengths already present in Oak Hills, and (4) getting everyone on the same page and assuming nothing.

The ANTS began their work underground but have continually "come up" to learn and to offer to carry the load, thereby enhancing and equipping the existing ministries and leaders God had provided. In other words, their underground work never undermined existing ministries. They have been evaluating even while they have been engaged in ministry themselves. In their behind-the-scenes work they have continually offered to set people up for even greater success, and in so doing they have broken down walls of resistance before the resistance ever became an issue. The ANTS team models servant leadership by its very name, and its early diligence has already produced a well thought out assessment process.

St. Monica's Catholic Church
Santa Monica, California
www.stmonica.net
Senior Pastor: Monsignor Lloyd Torgerson
Coordinator of Volunteer Ministry: Dan Shanahan

St. Monica's could be considered a "maverick" within the Archdiocese of Los Angeles. Led by an innovative pastor with a heart for the people, church members are very intentional about being a welcoming and inclusive community of faith.

The coordinator of volunteer ministry and his team have focused first, and comprehensively, on the ministry of hospitality. In fact, hospitality has become one of the primary identifying characteristics of the parish—no small accomplishment for a church with 6,400 members and seven services every weekend. A primary goal of the hospitality ministry, served by over 160 people, was to create a First Contact Team (FCT) made up of people with the gift of hospitality and a heart for connecting new people as soon as they join the church.

New people are invited to stand during the worship service so they can be welcomed by the congregation as the service begins. After worship the presider makes an invitation to the entire congregation to visit the welcome table on the patio outside the church doors, where people can come and speak to someone face-to-face and receive a warm welcome, as well as obtain information about the parish. People are invited to fill out a card that asks for some very basic information that would help them become known to the parish. These cards immediately are passed to the FCT. The next step is a welcome phone call by a team member to answer any questions they might have. The team is trained to make these ministry calls. All new people receive an invitation to attend an orientation to learn more about the church, meet the monsignor, and determine if they would like to commit to a relationship with the parish.

Everyone receives and is invited to fill out a ministry opportunities questionnaire in advance of a ministry placement interview. (Forms support all levels of connections at St. Monica's and are managed centrally by the office of volunteer ministry.) The next-level interview team, also trained for its task, begins the process of listening, discovering, and assessing with the person where he or she might serve best or have his or her needs met.

Sounds pretty simple and basic, doesn't it? But without the advocacy and voice of their leader, it would be impossible to carry out. The impact? People feel cared for rather than lost. After leaving an Interview Training Workshop at St. Monica's one day, I was speaking to a woman in the grocery store who asked where I had been. When I told her, her response affirmed what I already knew. She said, "Something is going on there! I don't know just what, but everybody seems to be so glad when a new person comes. It is a very special place."

QUESTIONS FOR REFLECTION AND DISCUSSION

1. Once a new member joins the church, how do you maintain his or her relationship to the church and cultivate his or her ongoing development?

2. What is your process to equip, recognize, and care for leaders in your church?

3. Are you seeking input from those serving in ministry? If not, why not?

4. What is your exit-interview process for leaders, and how do you follow up on the information you gather?

6

Launching the Vision

The gifts he gave were that some would be apostles, some prophets, some evangelists, some pastors and teachers, to equip the saints for the work of ministry, for building up the body of Christ, until all of us come to the unity of the faith and of the knowledge of the Son of God, to maturity, to the measure of the full stature of Christ.

Ephesians 4:11–13 NRSV

GIFTS COME IN VARIOUS sizes, forms, and packages. Gifts are a significant way to show love. In fact, one of the essential characteristics of love is the capacity to give. We give (to paraphrase 1 John 4:19) because God first gave to us.

The central importance of giving become clearer to me when I began to look at the context of our key equipping Bible passage and examine *gifts* in the letter to the Ephesians. My NRSV Exhaustive Concordance (I discovered what the title meant the first time I tried to pick it up) lists a number of uses of *gifts* and *giving* to describe an aspect of God's relationship with us (verses cited are from the New Revised Standard Version):

- I pray that the God of our Lord Jesus Christ, the Father of glory, may give you a spirit of wisdom and revelation as you come to know him (Ephesians 1:17).
- For by grace you have been saved through faith, and this is not your own doing; it is the gift of God (Ephesians 2:8).
- Of this gospel I have become a servant according to the gift of God's grace that was given me by the working of his power. Although I am the very least of all the saints, this grace was

given to me to bring to the Gentiles the news of the boundless riches of Christ (Ephesians 3:7–8).

- But each of us was given grace according to the measure of Christ's gift. Therefore it is said, "When he ascended on high he made captivity itself a captive; he gave gifts to his people" (Ephesians 4:7–8).
- The gifts he gave were that some would be apostles, some prophets, some evangelists, some pastors and teachers, to equip the saints for the work of ministry, for building up the body of Christ (Ephesians 4:11–12).
- Pray also for me, so that when I speak, a message may be given to me to make known with boldness the mystery of the gospel (Ephesians 6:19).

The main points I get from all these verses have to do with the source of who I am as a believer in Jesus and what I can do as his follower. The helplessness I referred to in the early chapters of this book has taught me over and over that I don't originate things in this world. They don't begin with me. I get to participate, both as a recipient and as a channel of God's grace. The more I learn about God's roles and responsibilities, the less I am prone to take over in areas that belong to him. When I don't have to be in charge of everything, I am free to enjoy the wonder that God allows me to participate at all!

Among God's many priceless gifts is the fact that he gave us to each other. I've learned through my children that one of the ways we know a gift is genuine is when it fits. I'm not just talking about a family in which we know each other so well that we get the right size when we buy clothes for each other—though I do consider that a minor miracle of love. I am thinking about those gifts of little or no material value that are nevertheless priceless: a note written to a parent or child, which they know could only have been meant for them, a gesture or word whose timing speaks volumes about the way someone understands us. The more attentive I am, the more I see God doing just that through the body of Christ. God fills my life with gifts I didn't know I needed, but which fit in such a way that I know they were given with me in mind by someone who knows me better than I know myself. I love the body of Christ not only because I fit in it but because it fits me too.

THE LAUNCH

THOSE FIRST EIGHTEEN MONTHS of trial-and-error ministry were some of the longest in my life. Moments of breakthrough that seemed too short were separated by long days of painfully slow progress. I have since learned through observation and cooperation that genuine, healthy change has a schedule of its own. The time we spent laying the groundwork for change in our church actually turned out to be relatively short. I can now truthfully say that I'm glad it took as long as it did. I'm thankful for each delay and setback, because I now realize that many of those obstacles that blocked my path and drove me to tears of frustration actually kept me from going in the wrong direction.

The groundwork we laid in the areas of biblical teaching, language change, system change, and cultural change eventually led to a launch point. As we saw the vision of life as an equipping church spread throughout the congregation, we realized that some kind of public beginning would be valuable.

Our pastor, Charles, actually brought up the necessity of a launch point early in our transition months. He knew that my appointment as the director of lay ministries hadn't made much of an impact on the awareness of the congregation at large. That was fine with me. I was working from the inside out, laying groundwork, desperately trying to uncover the pieces God had given us to carry out his work in his way at Brentwood. I think, looking back, that I was assuming we would gradually evolve into an equipping church.

Charles saw the transition differently. He saw the bigger picture. He wisely realized that challenges, little crises, and celebrations were as much a part of change as were careful analysis, wise planning, and gradual adjustments. His vision had room for the individual, but he also saw the church as an organic whole. Although he certainly taught that the Bible's guidelines for equipping ministry place a high value on the unique role of every individual member in the body, he also held before his staff members the exciting picture of the whole body functioning together.

In small ways, the vision was beginning to take root. My little team was actively observing the church, developing systems, and undertaking small experiments to discover what old ways still worked and what new ways might work better. Charles kept the larger questions before us: "How do we tell the congregation what is going on? How do we help them see not just miscellaneous little changes here and there, but the vision of what we can be together as a church? How do we tell *everyone* what some of us are learning?"

After a string of probing questions like these, he had a way of turning to me in our meetings and asking, "What do you have in mind?" The question was a little unnerving. I knew he was asking me for suggestions and direction in an area I was still assuming was his alone. I also knew he was right. He was leading by allowing and encouraging change to

---

**"How do we tell the congregation what is going on?
How do we help them see not just miscellaneous
little changes here and there, but the vision
of what we can be together as a church? How do
we tell *everyone* what some of us are learning?"**

---

occur, and he wanted to provide a model as our pastor/teacher in helping us as a group to understand and appreciate the process through which God was taking us. Every time he asked us that question he was letting go a little. What continually amazed us was that the more he let go of his stereotypical pastoral duties, the more we saw his real heart as a pastor coming through.

At first, my answer to his question about what I had in mind for us to do and for him to teach was little more than a shoulder shrug. I didn't have an answer. Creative worship and pastoral instruction were not my gifts. I knew I wanted as many of our church members as possible to share the equipping model and the serving attitude I was discovering everywhere in Scripture. I was passionate about what I wanted them to experience, and I knew what I wanted them to feel, but I didn't have the gifts to take them there myself.

As I have discovered again and again, my places of helplessness are places where God offers help. His help usually comes in the form of brothers and sisters in Christ—other members of the body. Although I did not possess the gifts of developing creative worship, I knew people who did. I thought of one woman in particular who was not only creative but also had an obvious passion for creative worship. She was the friend who invited us to visit Brentwood three years earlier. I had been aware of her passion for the church, knowing that her gifts of worship design had helped the church during the months before Charles arrived when the church had to function without a senior pastor.

I called Jaye and asked her to do some worship brainstorming with me. As providence would have it, both of us were signed up for an all-church ski trip and were going to travel together. Our first planning session lasted the whole five-hour car drive to the mountains. The time flew by. I filled her in on my recent spiritual education. I shared Charles's questions and concerns with her. I tried to paint a picture in words of our vision of the equipping church.

From the moment I began to tell my story I knew I had a soul mate. Her responses told me she understood. As I described our biblical discoveries and our hopes, she began to make suggestions. I sat amazed as I heard her take what had been powerful ideas and dreams for me and begin to say them back in the form of pictures, symbols, and corporate experiences. She took my words and gave them back to me as worship.

Jaye and I agreed that the greatest challenge would be to convey to the congregation that equipping ministry was not just a passing fad or the latest brainchild of our pastor. They needed to hear that even though the vision of equipping might sound new, it was really as old as the New Testament. We began to think of our launch as a congregational renewal, an act in which we claimed again the life God wanted us to enjoy.

I distinctly remember telling Jaye that I wanted the congregation to learn about spiritual gifts, but that they needed more than a biblical "brain dump" of facts about and descriptions of spiritual gifts. I wanted them to see and feel the impact of the gifts in people's lives. Using her understanding of Scripture and her creative wisdom, Jaye was able to translate my concerns into an effective worship plan. She was able to preserve the emphasis on biblical teaching while attending to the felt needs of the congregation. Our equipping launch became a matter of the head, heart, and soul.

They needed more than a biblical "brain dump" of facts about and descriptions of spiritual gifts. I wanted them to see and feel the impact of the gifts in people's lives.

DESIGN AND CULTURE

ONE OF THE CHARACTERISTICS of our church culture at Brentwood involves a long-standing pattern of teaching through storytelling. It has always been one of the distinct components we wouldn't want to change. Our relational closeness depended on sharing faith stories with each other. It still does. Our congregation seems to open her arms to those who get personal.

After rereading that paragraph, I realize I've intentionally chosen some words that might not carry the same weight in another church culture that they carry in ours. I could have used the term *testimony* instead of *faith story*. What I've heard others call witnessing, we have described as spiritual storytelling. These words speak more to context than content. Jaye understood the points of vulnerability in our congregation's worship pattern. She knew what doors to use to get through to our people. Finding the doors through which communication flows in your congregation will largely determine how clearly you convey any idea. I'm convinced that the doors of communication in your congregation are there and that if you don't know where they are, someone does. Locate a "door-keeper," and listen carefully to this person.

By the end of our five-hour drive to the Eastern Sierras, Jaye described for me how our launch would look and feel in the sanctuary at Brentwood. I tweaked her ideas a little, but I knew she had the right picture. I suggested to her some of the specific gifts and teaching we wanted to emphasize, and together we began to list the kinds of stories we wanted the congregation to hear. The more we brainstormed, the more excited we got about the upcoming months.

I don't remember much about what the skiing was like. I was anxious to get back to church. I now had a much clearer answer to my pastor's question, "What do you have in mind?" When we got back, Jaye and I met with Charles and explained our thoughts and plans. With his endorsement, we shared the plan with the entire staff. We had enough of a plan to give everyone some direction, but not so much plan that we left anyone out. We needed their input. We insisted on their suggestions and contributions.

We had enough of a plan to give everyone some direction, but not so much plan that we left anyone out. We needed their input. We insisted on their suggestions and contributions.

The series of worship experiences we planned was different from anything our congregation had ever done before. The pastoral staff, the minister of music, and many other church members would be called on to help launch the whole church into the vision of living as an equipping body of believers. We were modeling it as we preached it. In fact, the more we planned, the wider the participating group grew to become. I was discovering that the more people became involved in shaping and bringing events, projects, and programs into the life of the church, the more they became committed to helping them succeed. It makes sense, doesn't it? When we help design something, we own part of it. The plan becomes part of us. I've watched the principle demonstrated with delightful regularity in our church.

The music for the launch series represented a crucial component. Jaye and I had both sung in the choir for years. We worked closely with Jack Walker, our minister of music. He and Jaye chose music that would celebrate the gifts we were highlighting. The songs emphasized the ministry of the people. When we could not locate the right song to fit with the preaching themes, Jack wrote wonderful original music that enhanced our worship. I continually saw God use the ministry of many to teach many others about the ministry of many more.

By design, the launch sermon series began the Sunday after Easter and culminated on Pentecost Sunday. What better way to celebrate the place and power of spiritual gifts in the life of the church than to end the series on the Sunday we honor the giving of the Giver of the gifts.

THE GIVING TREE

THAT YEAR THE TRADITIONAL post-Easter downturn in attendance never had a chance to take root. Enough people had participated in the preparations for the launch series that the curiosity and interest levels were high. Something was going on, and people wanted to find out what it was.

The overarching biblical theme for the seven-week period was "You Are Gifted, You Are Called." Our central visual focus was "The Giving Tree." A member of the creative team came up with a large leafless birch tree that welcomed the congregation from the front of the sanctuary on the first Sunday of the series. The empty branches raised questions. It clearly did not fit among the live plants and cut flowers that often graced our worship space. Almost immediately people began to refer to it fondly as "our naked tree."

Charles acknowledged the chuckles as he introduced the tree. "In the weeks to come, you are going to see this tree come to life. We know that it looks a little naked now, but if you watch and listen closely, you will see this tree fill out as people discover, explore, and share their spiritual gifts during our worship times."

In our typical order of worship, the children's message represents the first teaching segment. Our associate pastor, Bill Barnes, based his conversation with the kids on the book *The Giving Tree*. Bill gently shared the story with this mini-congregation and pointed out the importance of each person offering his or her gifts to others. The rest of us grown-up children listened in. The launch was underway.

Each week for the next six Sundays the pastors preached on spiritual gifts. Some of these sermons dealt with clusters of gifts, while others highlighted individual gifts. The music before and after each sermon emphasized the "willing" aspects of the Christian life, because gift awareness makes little sense apart from encouragement to use the gifts in practical and effective ways. Therefore, every Sunday we included a musical piece by a talented church member who was exercising that particular gift for the first time. These were people with "untapped" gifts we had identified in our discovery process. They were asked to participate in this particular way as an added aspect of the teaching series. Most of them probably would not have responded to an open invitation to contribute a song in the worship service, but our level of awareness of individual abilities and interests was already expanding enough that we were

> **Gift awareness makes little sense apart from encouragement to use the gifts in practical and effective ways.**

able to make tactical specific invitations. These "new gifts" touched the congregation deeply.

The different people who shared their faith each Sunday challenged the rest of the church in unforgettable ways. Their words drove home with a simple eloquence the importance of the priesthood of all believers. For each service I asked individuals to speak who were using the gifts we were highlighting that Sunday or who had been served by those using those particular gifts. I asked each one to tell his or her story.

For those who were telling us their stories of faith we added a surprise feature. We arranged to have each person introduced by someone who had been touched by or benefited from that person's service. On the Sunday when we highlighted the gift of teaching, we invited Helen to speak. Helen had been active in the church for nearly fifty years and had been instrumental in developing our first Sunday school. Our initial nursery school ministry had been her idea. I asked her to share some of the impact on her own life that had come as a result of the years of practicing her spiritual gift of teaching.

Introducing Helen was a man in his forties whose life she had significantly touched. Bill had participated in Sunday school in the years before we had a Christian Education building. He described in touching detail all the ways Helen had made him feel special and useful, noting how each Sunday she had welcomed him early and asked him to put a Bible on each chair as they prepared the makeshift Sunday school rooms in a rented facility across the street from the church. Bill then went on to mention the impact of some of his Sunday school teachers who were dentists and how they served as effective models of what it meant to be a Christian man, husband, and father. He confessed that it shouldn't have come as a surprise when years later their impact revealed itself in his choice of a career, namely, dentistry. Bill's story had a powerful effect as he eloquently affirmed Helen's faithfulness. We all went away with a beautiful example of the full circle of ministry in which one generation blesses the next and is honored in turn for their labor.

Several weeks later we had as our theme the cluster made up of mercy, serving, and helps. Over a year earlier we had faced adversity as a congregation when a member's young husband committed suicide, leaving behind a devastated wife with the difficult prospect of raising a young son alone. Up until the tragedy, Andrea had been one of our leaders in children's ministry. She was used to being on the giving end rather than on the receiving end of service. As we were planning the launch series, I had lunch one day with Andrea and asked her if she would consider sharing her story. I told her it would mean a lot to hear how much the generous practice of spiritual gifts by some church members had affected her and her son's life. At first she was reluctant. She wasn't at all sure she wanted to relive those lonely days of grief. She eventually agreed to speak, and later she reported that the process of reflection turned out to produce a wonderful healing effect in her.

When Andrea stood before our congregation, her simple courage brought some to tears before she even said a word. She spoke with a gripping passion. "I could not have survived," she declared, "without the wise practical gifts exercised by members of this church following the tragedy that overwhelmed me. Some of you applied the ministry of paper plates, stocking my kitchen with disposable items so I wouldn't have to wash dishes. Others brought food for our immediate needs and then filled my freezer with meals for later." She went on to thank those—many who had come and gone without drawing attention to themselves—who had made life bearable by their practical help. She thanked those who had answered her phone so she could have some private moments, as well as those who had polished her son's shoes and laid out his clothes so he would have an outfit to wear at his father's memorial service.

A quiet and holy stillness settled over our sanctuary as Andrea continued. She thanked the men of the church who faithfully showed up week after week to continue a habit her son, Stephen, and his dad had established of spending Saturday mornings at the park. She recalled the women who came alongside and helped address thank-you notes when she found the task impossible. She went on and on, describing things that had been simple acts of kindness to those doing them, but a lifeline for her.

We were awakening to the truth that some gifts might be lying dormant or poorly used within our congregation, and we left that Sunday determined not to miss opportunities to exercise those gifts.

When Andrea returned to her seat, Charles stepped up to preach with tears in his eyes. "I don't know what I can add," he said tenderly. Andrea's story made a lasting impression. We had gathered to think about mercy, serving, and helps; instead, we witnessed and felt the amazing impact of those gifts applied in a terrible situation. We were awakening to the truth that some gifts might be lying dormant or poorly used within our congregation, and we left that Sunday determined not to miss opportunities to exercise those gifts. I could almost see the question in people's eyes as they looked at each other with a new sense of honor and attention: How many other Andreas were sitting in our pews that day?

VISUAL ARTS AND CREATIVE TEAMS

THE CREATIVE TEAM that worked on the plans for the launch series prepared carefully for the close of each worship service. We discussed how to offer the congregation an opportunity to respond to and affirm the gifts about which we were teaching.

Long before the launch series began, two teams of people who loved to create visual effects pondered how best to emphasize the teaching points of the pastors and teachers. One team created beautiful large banners to hang in the sanctuary. These illustrated the weekly gifts and added stunning texture and color to our worship space. As the preaching series progressed, the collection of banners became an impressive reminder of all the gifts that are present each time we gathered. The other team spent hours of fellowship creating thousands of finely crafted leaves (with hangers) that would adorn our naked birch tree.

These two teams illustrated what I call "the range of gift use" that characterizes an equipping church. Some people have gifts of professional-level quality. For example, we have in our church some excellent artists who make priceless contributions to our congregational life, while we also have many artistic people scattered all across the skill range who can produce an amazing variety of objects as they work together. The process of making leaves or banners offered many opportunities for participation. Everyone does not and cannot do everything. The artist who dreams up and sketches the idea for a banner may not be able to choose the type of fabrics that should be used. Others may be enlisted because of their embroidery or sewing skills. Meanwhile, a large group of people may be cutting out leaves that someone else has carefully drawn. A key assumption at Brentwood is that God works in and through people who work together.

Because artistic gifts are not part of my gift mix, I watched in wonder as paper and linen became stirring symbols of our life together and a vivid reminder of the many gifts God gives. I was reminded of what things must have been like in the wilderness of Sinai after God gave the people instructions for building the first tabernacle of worship. He gave them a blueprint and specific directions—but he also gave them gifts, wrapped in people, to accomplish his design:

Then the LORD said to Moses, "See, I have chosen Bezalel son of Uri, the son of Hur, of the tribe of Judah, and I have filled him with the Spirit of God, with skill, ability and knowledge in all kinds of crafts—to make artistic designs for work in gold, silver and bronze, to cut and set stones, to work in wood, and to engage in all kinds of craftsmanship. Moreover, I have appointed Oholiab son of Ahisamach, of the tribe of Dan, to help him."

Exodus 31:1–6

We had our own "descendants" of Bezalel and Oholiab at Brentwood. In preparing for the launch I never picked up a needle or scissors; others made those important contributions where my participation would have taken me outside my primary gifts. I had plenty of opportunities to keep my gifts busy, working with my own partners in planning, praying, and preparing in other ways for the launch. But I must admit there were moments of envy when I would walk past a room in the church and overhear the laughter and hum of conversation as people enjoyed each other's fellowship and served the Lord. Those feelings were invariably swept away by a tidal wave of joy as I reflected on what God was creating out of us. Besides, when my team got together, the fellowship was dynamic and inspiring, too. Those walking past our door must have wondered if we were getting anything done, since it seemed as though all we were doing was laughing!

COMMISSIONED FOR MINISTRY

THE WORK OF THE creative arts teams had a dramatic effect on the close of every worship service in the series. We identified and commissioned the gifts that had been presented during the service, and then Charles or one of the other pastors would invite all who realized they'd been given gifts of that particular type to come forward. Each person was presented with a handcrafted leaf to adorn the branches of the giving tree. These were powerful moments of invitation and affirmation.

In preparation for these times, we made a special effort to compile lists of every conceivable version and application of the highlighted gifts. We particularly looked for ways in which gifts were being used beyond the boundaries of our church. Our launch was to be a celebration of the way in which believers use their gifts in all of life. These worship times brought the gifts together for clarification, encouragement, and expansion, then sent out the possessors of these gifts to function in ministries of Jesus Christ.

From the start we practiced the understanding that if believers are equipped with direction to use their God-given spiritual gifts, the local church will not be able to contain the energy that will be released. Even a large church cannot include enough internal opportunities for the gifts to be exercised. Gifts are given to reach out to the world!

Our equipping church lifestyle emphasized the biblical truth that evangelism flows from the use of gifts. People often come to Jesus Christ because a disciple of Jesus has served them. The community desperately needs believers who will exercise their gifts wherever God has placed them.

Thus, for example, on the Sunday during which we celebrated the gift of teaching, Charles listed an astonishing array of teaching applications that were represented in our church. He called forward those who taught in our Sunday school and in public schools. Trainers in business settings and special instructors of all different kinds were invited to come. Counselors, disciplers, mentors, and many others were identified—as many roles as possible that served in these different settings for the gift of teaching.

On the Sunday the gift cluster of mercy, serving, and helps was highlighted, a list was read that included nurses, care providers, nursing-home workers and visitors, family caregivers, and participants in Stephen ministries and hospice care. We saw people beginning to identify gifts in each other, and we found that people often hesitated to claim a gift in themselves until someone came along and affirmed the gift, having seen or experienced the gift in practice.

Week after week, people streamed forward and hung their "gift leaves" on the once-naked tree. They acknowledged their participation in the whole. Soon the tree was covered with these expressions. A visual symbol of what we could look like together gradually emerged.

On Pentecost Sunday, the launch series reached its conclusion. We prayed and planned for an event God would use to alter the course of our church. This was to be the final step in a dance of transformation we had been practicing for seven weeks. The leaf team that helped us dress our naked tree had designed still another expressive component. They created hundreds of small clusters of cherries, which would be added to the giving tree and represent the fruit of the Spirit. The biblical text for the day was Galatians 5:22–23: "But the fruit of the Spirit is love, joy, peace, patience, kindness, goodness, faithfulness, gentleness and self-control. Against such things there is no law."

Charles preached on the fruitful spiritual results that come from the exercise of our gifts. We celebrated the Lord's Supper together following the message. As the congregation came forward to partake of the bread and juice, each member hung their cluster of fruit on the tree. These actions allowed us to express our desire to experience whatever

God's Spirit wanted to bring forth from our gifts. The gifts were from the Holy Spirit; so was the fruit.

Our once-naked birch tree now stood fully clothed in leaves and fruit, reminding us that as we offered our gifts back to the One who gave them, the Spirit would create from them a wonderful harvest to the glory of God. A sense of awe and expectation filled our sanctuary that day. No, we didn't see the flames of Acts 2—but God's presence was unmistakable.

NEW WAYS WITH QUESTIONNAIRES

IMMEDIATELY FOLLOWING EACH of the morning services on that Pentecost Sunday we enjoyed a meal together. During that meal a specially trained team began to do its work. I had identified people who could interview and gather information, and they launched a concerted effort to update the information we had on our church membership.

Up to this point, most of our information centered on geography and biography. Because we were determined to function as an equipping church, we needed as much gift-oriented information as possible. We wanted to know about our members' past church involvement (the ways they had actively served in the past). Where were they currently serving in the community? What areas of service interested them? How would they describe their skills? What experiences had they gone through that might serve as preparation for some new ministry?

The questions did not come as a surprise to them. Previously I had mailed out questionnaires to all church members, with a cover letter signed by Charles and me, informing them that Pentecost Sunday would be the official ribbon-cutting launch of lay ministries in our church. I acknowledged the progress we had already made but encouraged them to think about the need to have a "whole church coming together" moment. I reminded them that the questionnaires would help us as we planned teaching topics, matched opportunities with gifts and interests, and responded to special needs. At strategically located interview tables we received back the questionnaires during the brunches. The ground-work of the launch series gave everyone a sense that the information they were now supplying would significantly advance our efforts to be an equipping church.

EQUIPPING PRINCIPLES

A Launch Is Necessary

Although the process of transformation into an equipping church will involve many changes along the way, an important milestone will be missed if a launch of the biblical model isn't held at some point. The decision even to begin to move toward becoming an equipping church will require the support of the pastor and the key leaders of the church. A lot of foundational biblical teaching will have to come from the pulpit. The studies and structural rearrangements I've discussed will have to have been undertaken. Everything won't be done, but don't launch the vision without the basics already in place.

As I've noted elsewhere, without a launch in which the entire church participates, the equipping model becomes just another program tacked on to the existing church structure—with much-diminished effectiveness.

A Launch Should Be Timed

Now that I've walked through this process with a number of churches, I can say with some degree of certainty that the timeline for an effective launch must include at least eighteen months to two years of intentional groundwork. Leaders who are not committed to this length of development time are, by and large, looking for a quick fix, not a dynamic transformation of their church.

About a year into the process, begin to project a launch date. On a parallel track with the development of the system infrastructure, establish some key objectives leading up to that date, asking questions such as:

- When will the preparatory sermon series begin?
- What is the best time of the year for us to do this?
- What key teams need to be identified and invited to help develop the launch?
- When will our systems be ready to receive the information that will come with churchwide discovery?

Launch Is Spelled T-E-A-M-S

If you cannot invite a significant number of people to participate in specific roles in planning the launch of equipping ministries, then you are not ready to launch. Several teams are crucial in the planning process—worship, creative arts, interview, tracking systems, along with many others.

The wisdom we discovered at Brentwood is that the launch itself was just the icing on the cake we'd been baking for months as teams planned the event and as Charles laid the biblical foundation for the direction we were heading. We invited such a high percentage of the membership to help plan the launch that a commitment to equipping ministry was at a fever pitch by the time the launch actually occurred.

Some of the teams that have formed for the purpose of planning the launch will have ongoing duties during and after the launch. The interview team got a workout the weekend of the launch and for many days thereafter. They loved it! Why? Because we invited them to do what they loved to do! The same was true of the other teams.

In the process of planning for the launch you will learn more about team building than I could write about in several books. You will learn about teams in your particular situation. You and your key team will learn about some right ways and some wrong ways to invite people into ministry. You will learn that people sometimes volunteer for things they really don't like at all. You will have the wonderful challenge of inviting them to consider doing something else that would fit their gifts and talents.

If you haven't made the shift from committees to teams when you visualize your church, then you are probably not yet ready to launch an equipping model.

EQUIPPING HEROES

First Presbyterian Church of Bellevue
Bellevue, Washington
www.fpcbellevue.org
Senior Pastor: Richard Leon
Director of Lay Ministries: Ginny Hall

When Ginny Hall began her work at First Presbyterian, her top priority was building a strong core team to facilitate the vision of equipping ministries. Recognizing the unique gifts needed to create all the elements of the process, Ginny built the first core team under the leadership of cochairs, and this team flourished. She duplicated this pattern by choosing two gifted leaders for each new area of development. As a facilitating leader, Ginny recognized from the beginning that it was important to model that the process not be centered on any one individual.

Based on the theory that two heads are better than one, shared leadership had a number of advantages. New leaders always had a partner to lean on and learn from in the course of doing the hard work. In spite of busy schedules, one leader would invariably be available when the other wasn't. The process of obtaining commitments was easier because every candidate knew that he or she would be sharing the load. The number of people in leadership training doubled right from the start, and when individuals moved away or chose to take on other responsibilities, there was less of a vacuum to be filled.

While some of the names and functions of the team have changed over time, the initial core team developed the following subministry teams to accomplish the overall mission:

- The Interview team (which became the Small Group Leaders team): to plan and carry out interviews to discover gifts and place people in ministry
- The Ministry Connection team: to support all the ministries
- The Gift Discovery team: to create a unique assessment tool responsive to the church culture and to establish a class on spiritual gifts
- The Ministry Opportunities team: to focus on ministry descriptions and identify places to serve
- The Publicity and Promotions team (which became the Communications team): to advertise the gift classes and to lift up the people who are regularly doing ministry
- The Computer Support team: to create and run the systems that support the process
- The Appreciation and Recognition team: to honor all those in ministry
- The Leadership Development team (the latest addition): to develop curriculum to respond to the needs of new and current leaders

The strengths of this model are many. The core team created an authentic model of a gift-based leadership team. Very quickly it elevated the value for team and lay ministries in the church as the rest of the staff saw the collaborative spirit and accomplishments of the group. The teamwork was inspiring and contagious. While the vision took a great deal of time and hard work to implement, the results have been worth the effort. The satisfaction in the level of ownership on the part of this team is extraordinary.

QUESTIONS FOR REFLECTION AND DISCUSSION

1. Reflect back on your launch sermon series. Did it have the desired outcomes? How could you have improved it for the next time?

2. Who has a story to share that exemplifies the transformational impact of serving out of their giftedness? Make a list. Invite them to share their heart.

3. In what ways are you keeping the vision alive in your people?

4. How regularly do you recast the equipping vision?

5. Reflect on your teaching "language." Does it continually call out the people of God as the ministers of the church?

7

Discovering Gifts, Talents, and Experience

και αυτος εδωκεν τους μεν αποστολους, τους δε προφητας,
τους δε ευαγγελιστας, τους δε ποιμενας και διδασκαλους.

Ephesians 4:11–13 The Greek New Testament
(United Bible Societies Third Edition)

I KNOW YOU ARE probably mumbling, "Wow, that looks like Greek to me."
Yes, it is. Let me assure you that I can't read it, but I have friends who
can. One of them recently recited aloud Ephesians 4:11 in Greek. I was
surprised! The Greek words for some of the key equipping roles sounded
very familiar—*apostolous* (apostles), *prophētas* (prophets), *euangelistas*
(evangelists). Even my untrained ear had to admit they looked and
sounded suspiciously like the English words in my Bible.

Well, my friend wasn't done with me. He told me that those who
first translated the Greek New Testament into English decided in certain cases to borrow Greek terms rather than to translate them. As he
explained it to me, this is called *transliterating*. It happens when a translator's guiding principle is the creation of a "one word for one word" version from one language to another. Sometimes the new language doesn't
have a specific term or name for an object or role; in such cases the original word may be borrowed and lifted into the target language. Personal
names, for example, are often transliterated. A translator's other choice
requires the use of a descriptive phrase instead of a single word to get the
meaning across. In that case, the translation of the "role" words above **101**

might end up looking like: "He gave some to be his living representatives [apostles], some to help people apply God's Word [prophets], some to share the good news [evangelists]." If the context doesn't clearly supply an explanation of the word, a definition has to be given sooner or later. A significant part of Christian teaching involves the explanation of transliterated words.

What does all this have to do with the equipping church? The more I go back (or in this case, am guided back) to the Scriptures, the more I find that they describe what we long to experience in Christ's body. The terms we are talking about are among the essential roles in the church. Significant gifts and duties within the body of Christ are sometimes neglected because the terms simply are not understood or have been so sanctified that we cannot imagine they apply in the present at all. Yet, once we agree that there will never be another of the original apostles, can we not also agree that at least some part of the role the apostles played in the early church still needs to be carried out today? So too, does the church today no longer need prophetic voices?

Working alongside, and sometimes weeping with, pastors has allowed me to discover that many of them had little opportunity to do the work of self-discovery (you see, it wasn't a required part of their seminary education). They have seldom been encouraged to determine their spiritual gifts, their leadership style, and what motivates them to behave the way they do—and how all this significant self-discovery work impacts their role as pastors.

As a layperson I identify with many faithful church members who find it frustrating when their leaders can't seem to define and explain their own calling. Sometimes I think pastors are so busy trying to do what other people want them to do that they become paralyzed to declare what they are convinced God is calling them to do. How can laypeople develop confidence about their own call from God when their spiritual leaders don't model confidence in God's leading? I've been blessed to experience a church that does take seriously the opportunities and limitations of God's call on a person's life, and it has been an incomparable joy to participate in Christ's body in action. I've witnessed the freedom that our pastor experienced as his duties were narrowed and his ministry deepened.

VISION IN ACTION

THE LAUNCH OF THE equipping church vision at Brentwood Presbyterian did not play out a fairy tale. The special launch Sunday did not end with a voice from heaven declaring, "And they will now live happily ever after!" Even though a tremendous amount of work had gone on before the launch, that day itself marked merely the beginning of a long commitment to change—a commitment that continues to make a difference almost fifteen years later.

That Pentecost Sunday set the stage. It was as though we had spent the previous weeks reviewing what the Scripture said we ought to be, and along the way we discovered a lot about ourselves. But that final Sunday represented the choice in the road, the corporate change of direction. In a congregational sense, we gathered that day to affirm Joshua's words: "But as for me and my household, we will serve the LORD" (Joshua 24:15).

We had a long way to go. We didn't have much of a terminology to use, so we figured out the language as we went along. When Charles preached about our vision, he constantly used the clarifier "every member is a minister." He personalized the statement from the pulpit: "That means *you* are ministers!" He employed descriptive phrases, stories, and faith sharings that tied back to the biblical language of the priesthood of all believers.

In our case, the vision of the priesthood of all believers functioned much like Rick Warren's "purposes" in *The Purpose-Driven Church*— a book that continues to be recommended reading for anyone called to church planting. It articulates many of the same principles we discovered at Brentwood as we worked to place our church into a clearer biblical mold. We would have described ourselves as a church living into a biblical vision of the body of Christ.

Note the interesting parallel between Saddleback Valley Community Church and Brentwood Presbyterian Church. Rick Warren moved into the Mission Viejo area in Southern California and began his church in 1980; Charles Shields became pastor at Brentwood in 1981. These two pastors are representative of a much larger group of people who were shaping pastoral ministry at the time, determined to lead their churches in ways that were faithful to biblical teaching and effective at reaching people in our society. They and many others—Bill Hybels (Willow Creek Community Church), Wayne Cordeiro (New Hope Christian Fellowship), Mike Slaughter (Ginghamsburg United Methodist Church), Kirbyjon Caldwell (Windsor Village United Methodist Church), to name a few— have been pioneers. They have blazed a trail in church health and growth and have helped countless others by sharing their experiences. To some degree, anyone who sets out to follow Christ into a biblically consistent ministry will discover the truth of Rick Warren's confession:

> Very little of Saddleback's ministry was preplanned. I didn't have any long-range strategy before I started the church. I simply knew God had called me to plant a new church built on the five New Testament purposes, and I had a bag of ideas I wanted to try out. Each

innovation we've developed was just *a response* to the circumstances in which we found ourselves. I didn't plan them in advance. Most people think of "vision" as the ability to see the future. But in today's rapidly changing world, vision is also the ability to accurately assess current changes and take advantage of them. Vision is being alert to opportunities.[1]

There were, however, important differences between Saddleback and us. Rick Warren's original call was to plant a new church among unchurched people. His cultural sensitivity centered on understanding elements of the largely pagan culture into which he had moved. On the other hand, Charles was called to a church with an extensive history. Our cultural sensitivity centered on understanding a long-standing Christian tradition with deep roots. Rick had the challenge and joy of helping create a new church culture; we had the challenge and joy of transforming an existing church culture. Rick had to grow his leadership from scratch; we had to scratch our leadership where they itched, and then make sure they were leading in places that fit their gifts for spiritual growth.

Much more could be said about these differences. The essence of what they teach, however, is that every church that seeks to follow the biblical pattern will produce an original version. The principles we uncovered that influence the development of an equipping church will offer you guidelines. You can find them where we did, namely, in the Scriptures. But the ways in which we applied these principles are unique to our church setting. Some will work in your setting; many won't.

AFTER THE LAUNCH

As I NOTED IN the last chapter, we began a major push on launch Sunday to gather useful information for lay mobilization. In the years since we began this process a lot of work has been done in this area, and there are abundant resources for churches that wish to undertake serious mobilization. You will find some of these resources listed on the Leadership Training Network Web site at www.ltn.org.

In our equipping church model *discovery* has become the term we use to describe the adventure of finding out the scope of each person's gifts, talents, and experience. We note what this person is prepared to contribute to the whole. Along the way, we also uncover needs. Holistic discovery involves a balance between resources and needs. It sees people with marvelous potential for service without overlooking the difficulties

---

[1]Rick Warren, *The Purpose-Driven® Church* (Grand Rapids: Zondervan, 1995), 27–28.

or obstacles that might prevent them from serving. Healthy discovery remembers that while Jesus served without demanding to be served, his life modeled a continual ebb and flow of serving and being served.

Without balance, marvelous opportunities for ministry can be missed. My good friend and partner in ministry Calvie Hughson Schwalm, who currently serves as director of volunteer ministries at the Crystal Cathedral in Garden Grove, California, told me a classic story about the benefits of balance in discovery. This experience occurred in her previous work as director of lay ministries at a church in Orlando, Florida, and it left an indelible impact on her heart.

In the course of Calvie's duties she noted a young professional family who regularly attended the church. The husband was an up-and-coming corporate lawyer and the wife a teacher. Calvie discovered that they had recently moved into the area and planned to make her church their spiritual home. When she tried to set up an appointment to interview them for membership and participation information, the husband had trouble setting aside the time. Eventually, since Calvie is both creative and persistent, she volunteered to stop by his office for just a brief period of time and at least begin the conversation.

As Calvie was explaining the purpose of her visit, the young lawyer interrupted her with a concise comment. "I realize I've been hard to reach for this appointment, and frankly, I've been avoiding it. My wife and I were very active in our last church, and we're glad we've found a new church home so quickly here. I know your intentions in wanting this information are the best, and we fully plan to be active participants in the life of the church. But right now we can't."

Calvie, a well-trained listener, sensed that he was under tremendous strain, so she asked, as gently as she could, "I wonder if you have any needs we could pray about during this transition time?"

A tear ran down the young man's face as he said, "We know we're new and we haven't wanted to be a burden to the church, but we're desperate. Our little boy will be having a critical surgery next week, and we feel so alone."

Calvie was stunned. She had no idea of the stress in this young couple's life. She asked if they had told any of the pastoral staff about their situation. They hadn't, and she asked and received permission to do so. She also assured him that there were people in the church who would be eager to pray for them and their child and that their needs would not be "a burden," but a wonderful opportunity for church members to serve their newfound friends.

The focus of the rest of their conversation shifted to the specifics of their needs. The surgery was to take place in another city, which would create an added complication for their family in terms of travel plans. They had no way of knowing how long they would be gone.

As much as Calvie wanted to immerse herself in this couple's situation, her gifts as an administrator overruled. She returned to the church and set in motion an awesome display of compassion. Notifying the rest of the pastoral staff members, she called key people in the areas of prayer ministry and helps, providing each group with information specific to their roles.

Before the day was out, the young couple felt themselves lifted up by caring people. They sensed themselves surrounded by prayer. One of the pastors visited and made arrangements for a pastor to be with them at the hospital. A team promised to take over the management of their home while they were gone, doing the little upkeep tasks that a house requires. Meals and other practical necessities arrived on the scene to allow them to focus on travel preparations. A couple of people took care of getting them to the airport when the time came, and still others helped with many other details. All of the assistance was done in an orderly and gentle way by people who were doing what they were gifted to do. These were not delegated duties pulled out of a hat and assigned to whomever happened to be available, but opportunities to apply God-given abilities. The young couple later reported that they discovered during those days what belonging truly meant. Holding each other as they went to bed at night, they wept with relief and gratitude.

That story has several happy endings. The surgery for the child was successful. The family never felt alone during the long hours and days that followed. When they returned home, they joined the church and added their considerable skills, experiences, and character to the rest of the body. But the key to it all was a caring and persistent person who, in the middle of trying to get to know them, discovered a point of desperate need the church could meet.

DISCOVERY IS PERSONAL

DISCOVERY IS FAR MORE than a simple written inventory. It must be personal and include a face-to-face interview, as well as utilizing other methods and instruments. At the heart of discovery is an intentional conversation of the head and the heart that emphasizes listening. Some people are gifted in carrying on such conversations; they've been given one of the applications of the gift of discernment. Their ministry should be recognized and valued in the church for the guidance they can provide to those who need help in determining their needs as well as their gifts and skills.

At the heart of discovery is an intentional conversation of the head and the heart that emphasizes listening.

Discovery remains a work in progress. Information must be updated at every level. When people realize that the church takes this task seriously and uses the information effectively, they will be more likely to offer it willingly because they know that they will be equipped to serve in areas where they are gifted.

Discovery is labor-intensive, requiring many people. But effective lay mobilization does not happen without discovery. In fact, one key way to measure progress in lay mobilization is to ask, "How well are we doing discovery? How well do we know our people, their needs, their place on their spiritual journey, their challenges, their passions, their gifts, their interests, and their readiness to serve?"

DISCOVERY AND THE BIG PICTURE

DISCOVERY ALSO STEPS BACK from time to time to visualize the church as an organic whole. The process seeks to recognize the group strengths and resources as well as the overall needs that develop. In order for the connection to be effective, discovery must produce a sense of both individual and corporate resources and needs. Discovery creates effective profiles for individuals within the church, but it also develops a continually changing profile for the whole church.

This can be as simple as recognizing that a huge untapped source of wisdom and energy resides with those who may be extremely limited in their ability to move about. One person overseeing a ministry of transportation can often be the answer to unleashing a small army of people who have time to offer but have had no way to get there. Or to use an example that influenced my own life, for years at Brentwood a significant percentage of our secretarial needs were met by volunteers who took specific parts of those job descriptions and faithfully carried them out. We've had a "Volunteer of the Day" opportunity that has opened doors of practical service to those who have the qualifications but have limited time.

DISCOVERY AND THE WORLD

DISCOVERY MUST ALSO INCLUDE the world beyond the doors of the church. The gifts within a church will not be fully used if their application is limited to what can be done within the church. If a key purpose of the gifts is to build up the church, and if the built-up church results from people moving out of the kingdoms of this world and into the kingdom of God, then many of the gifts have an evangelistic application. They will affect people on the outside. Three stories from our experience at Brentwood illustrate this truth.

Robert

In Los Angeles the blessings of our climate make it possible for people to live without shelter year-round; thus, we have a number of homeless people in our area of town. But the fact that we share our good weather with the homeless doesn't begin to exhaust the opportunities we have to reach out with the love of Christ.

Balmy Sundays have typically allowed our church to host fellowship times out-of-doors. Our sun-dappled patio makes an ideal place for gathering before and after services to enjoy a snack and a cup of coffee or juice. Access to the street provides enough welcome that we've frequently had homeless persons stop in to share in the food and drink. They've been welcomed to stay for worship but have never been compelled.

Among the ranks of these transient visitors was a man named Robert, who gradually became a regular. Large in size and potent in aroma, Robert enjoyed the food, but also appreciated the kindness he was shown by people at the church. They remembered his name and made him feel welcome.

Eventually, and somewhat unexpectedly, Robert decided he wanted to become part of the church. First he stayed for worship once in a while. Then he told someone he really wanted to sing in the choir. This simple desire created some concern, as we were caught off-balance. We thought of Robert as someone who needed our help and our kindness, but it hadn't occurred to us that this could create an emotional debt that Robert might want to repay. What would it mean to have someone like Robert serving alongside us?

To his credit, our minister of music brought up Robert's situation at our staff meeting. He reported that the choir was experiencing some angst over Robert's participation—to which our pastor, Charles, responded, "Well, Jack, what do you see as the real problem?"

After a moment of uncertainty, Jack said, "I guess the problem is that he's dirty and he smells bad." He was telling the truth, because Robert had no home and no shower. It was one thing to greet him on the outdoor patio, but it was another thing to consider sharing the close confines of the choir loft.

Long before the WWJD bracelets had become popular, Charles asked us the essential question: "What do you think Jesus would have us do in this case?" A steely silence settled over the meeting. Robert's response to our welcome had created a challenge for the rest of us. How wide was our welcome? We all believed Jesus loved Robert. How much did we love him? The unspoken question was before us: "Do we talk and walk only a little of the right talk and walk, or do we go all the way in serving Jesus?"

We began to love Robert by praying for him. We talked about how we might accept him while at the same time recognizing that his presence presented real challenges. Eventually, the choir came up with a practical solution. Our minister of music took Robert aside and gave him a special orientation, gently explaining to him, "Robert, we would love to have you sing with us. Here is the guideline we all follow: If you want to sit up front, you will have to come clean on Sunday mornings. We also have a gift we want to give you to welcome you to the choir." They presented Robert with a complete Sunday outfit to wear. He became an official member of the choir.

For more than seven years now Robert has been a faithful participant in choir, wearing the same clothes every week, singing his heart out! He is a continual reminder of lessons we've learned and places we've been stretched to grow as a church. Robert, with single-hearted simplicity, took us all far beyond our comfort zone. And he wasn't done yet.

Early one day Robert showed up at my office before I arrived. He wanted to share with me a proposal for the church. I will never forget his simple expression of his idea. By this time, Robert had taken to calling the church his "family of faith" and using the term "brethren" when he spoke of other homeless people. He told me he thought our church ought to have a feeding program for his brethren.

"I still have brethren out there who need food," he said, "and we have a kitchen, and we have people who can cook. I'm not suggesting that we bring my brethren here, because some of them aren't very nice, and they're kind of angry. So I don't want them at the church. But down in Santa Monica where they eat, if we took the food down there, we could feed them."

As we talked a little more, I realized that he had thought through this plan very carefully. I confess I was amazed, and I was surely guilty of limiting Robert to first impressions. He had far more to offer than I realized. The church belonged to him, and he was demonstrating it by offering us to the world.

I called our mission elder and told him I had a man in my office with a proposal I thought was worthy of their attention. We arranged for Robert to appear at a meeting of the mission action group later in the week. Robert showed up in his Sunday clothes for what he considered a serious, godly mission. His hands shook while he held his paper and talked about his plan for feeding the homeless. The men and women of our mission team sat quietly attentive and humbled. Robert was eloquent because he was speaking from the heart about a dream that was becoming a vision. His compassion brought tears to the eyes of those who heard him that night. They decided without hesitation to have Robert present his proposal to the governing board of the church for approval.

This was the birth of the Brentwood Presbyterian Church "Saturday Evening Feeding" outreach to people without homes—a ministry that continues to this day. On Saturday mornings we prepare food in our kitchen and take it to Santa Monica to help feed the homeless. Robert understood and applied the biblical principle that from those who are given much, much is required. Robert made his "much" go a long way.

Who could have known that on some Sunday in the nearly forgotten past a homeless man would walk onto our patio and eventually become a visionary leader among us? God knew, and he set us up! As a church we have seen God repeatedly demonstrate that he loves to use the unqualified to do the unimaginable. God takes people who even we who should know better overlook and makes them his treasured servants.

As a church we have seen God repeatedly demonstrate that he loves to use the unqualified to do the unimaginable.

Jane

Like Robert, some people are overlooked in church because others think they have nothing to offer; others get passed over because it seems they have too much to offer. They are perceived as too busy, too affluent, or too committed to other things to be interested in church work. And if truth be told, the assumptions are right. If all we have to offer people is "church work," we shouldn't be surprised if they decline our invitation.

People need a compelling reason to become involved. The opportunities must fit their gifts, their interests, and their calling from God. If they can't see that their participation expresses some genuine compassion for others, even those who do serve will eventually lose interest. One of the central objectives of discovery is to improve our ability to match needs with people. Or to put it another way, we want to connect "people resources" with "people needs." Good discovery helps us care for each other more effectively.

Jane, whose gifts included the ability to raise large sums of money, was married to Todd, an outstanding orthopedic surgeon. She had helped raise millions of dollars for medical purposes in our area. Although Jane and her husband attended Brentwood, they had stayed somewhat on the periphery. During the process of discovery, her considerable leadership abilities were confirmed, and she was eventually asked to serve as the "elder to mission" in our church.

At this same time, Jane actively supported a capital campaign during which our church raised two million dollars. One of the guidelines for the campaign stated that we would earmark 25 percent of the funds for mission outreach. We made that decision before we raised any money. The implications and value of that decision took on a different tone when the figure was no longer 25 percent of some nebulous amount, but half a million dollars! It represented a new and significant commitment to mission in our church.

Half of the mission-targeted funds were designated to a Presbyterian mission hospital in Malawi, Africa, for the building of a pediatric wing. At one point during this several-years-long process we had a missions conference with a guest speaker from the umbrella ministry called the Medical Benevolence Foundation, which helps churches that undertake the kind of project we embraced. Jane and her husband opened their home to Ben Mathis, the special guest from the foundation—which began a long friendship.

Not being content to stay only partly informed, Jane and Todd soon signed up for a mission trip to Malawi to see firsthand the impact of our giving on the needs of that far-off place. What they witnessed changed their lives forever. They were overwhelmed by the needs of the people in Africa. As skilled observers with medical experience, they were horrified by some of the conditions and convinced that the church could do even more. They returned as champions for the cause of mission in our church.

Tragically, not long after they returned from Africa, Todd died. He had a history of heart disease and had undergone a number of bypass surgeries. We lost a skillful personal friend who had doctored all three of our children. But neither his youthfulness nor his own medical skill could overcome the effects of a weak heart. In the wake of this painful loss, Jane immersed herself in the needs of others, finding ways to honor Todd's desire to serve those in Africa.

I watched this elegant, graceful woman grow from being uncertain about her role in the church into being an effective leader for outreach. As an elder to mission, she was a tireless spokesperson for the importance of mission giving and going. She has marshaled her contacts in the outside community to raise significant amounts of money for the Medical Benevolence Foundation (where she eventually served as a board member) and for specific needs in Africa. Her considerable talents have been fueled by her passion for mission. We at Brentwood Presbyterian Church were honored to celebrate the transformation in her life as Jane assumed the ministry role of president of the Medical Benevolence Foundation.

Jane offers a wonderful example of the power of service to change the servant. She reminds us that Christ's servants come from every part of society. No one is too high or low to serve or to be served. In Christ there is an inexhaustible supply of opportunities for ministry.

Vision Meets Chaos: The Los Angeles Riots

In the summer of 1992 we found ourselves overwhelmed by what became known as the Los Angeles riots. As a storm of violence swept through our city, we spent a night of terror in the midst of fires, looting, and crime. There seemed to be no escape from the sounds and smells of a ravaged city.

When dawn finally broke, the stench of burned tires and torched buildings filled the air. Block after block of the city looked like the aftermath of all-out war. A question hung in the air, as heavy as the smoke that lingered after the fires: What would the new day bring?

It was not the government or the police who opened locked doors and stepped into the mean streets. Healing and calm began with the people of faith. Sometimes alone, and often in small groups, Christians, Jews, and Muslims left their homes and faced the nightmare. They prayed and wept with the wounded and the devastated. They took the first steps toward rebuilding the community simply by being present, long before a single brick was again laid or a window replaced.

The obvious task of cleanup brought together very different kinds of people. In working together, far more was accomplished than clearing debris from the streets. People of faith, doing what they could do, applied the healing salve of hope on the gaping wounds of the city.

In the early days of the healing, our church joined many other Anglo churches in partnerships with inner-city churches that had suffered damage during the riots. I had the privilege of participating in the task force created and called together by our presbytery the day after the riots. I was the only director of lay ministries in our community at the time.

Our first meeting was the single most painful experience I have been a part of during my life as a woman of faith. Everyone else there was a clergyperson—Korean, African-American, Hispanic, and Anglo pastors. We were all Presbyterians. My role was to listen for ways to mobilize people to support and serve some of the fifty-five churches in our presbytery who had been damaged or destroyed and to marshal outside resources to support further healing. I heard a group of men that day sharing the raw honesty of their recent and shocking awakening. They talked, argued, and eventually wept openly together.

> **How much more would the church of Jesus Christ
> accomplish if we listened more carefully
> to one another and to the world?**

The obvious truth I observed that day was that these men were discovering one another for the first time, for they had never previously made the effort. They were shockingly ignorant of each other's culture. The Koreans, who have a very quiet and reserved culture, discovered how they had unwittingly offended their African-American brothers, who resented the fact that Koreans would never look them in the eye—an action that in Korean culture was a sign of disrespect. The Koreans for their part had to admit to being uncomfortable with and even intimidated by the kind of warm, hands-on, high-five, enthusiastic encounters and interaction that is a part of African-American culture. It hurt to listen to these grown men sharing their stories and confronting their wrong assumptions about each other. Their failure to know each other and their reliance on misunderstood actions had created holy wars of separation from and bias against brothers and sisters in faith.

I learned volumes about reconciliation during those hours. I learned that it is important to share, but even more important to listen. These men had to pay a huge price in order to reach the place where they were finally able to hear each other. Until they really listened, their care for each other was extremely limited. But listening led to deeper understanding, and their new awareness made it possible for them to come alongside each other in ministry and to personally support each other in ways they had never thought about before.

How much more would the church of Jesus Christ accomplish if we listened more carefully to one another and to the world? What new approaches would we adopt if we started actively listening to Christ himself? Because the church was designed by Christ to be a place of grace, it can also be a wonderful training ground for listening.

VISION OVERCOMES CHAOS

BRENTWOOD'S PARTICIPATION IN THE aftermath of the Los Angeles riots had roots that preceded those difficult days. Back in the mid-1980s, Charles and I already had established a relationship with Pastor Leon Fanniel of St. Paul's Presbyterian Church, an African-American congregation affected by the riots. Several of us had visited Leon's church, and I had assisted with leadership training there on several occasions. In exchange, Leon had served as a mentor for me, giving me insight into

African-American perspectives and challenging my spiritual walk through his own deep humility and faithfulness.

I called Leon the day after the night of violence because Charles and I were concerned about his personal well-being and the condition of his church. Charles had encouraged me to ask Leon if there were ways we could join with them in promoting reconciliation, solidarity, and healing. We wanted to be among those who did whatever was necessary to prevent such a firestorm from ever engulfing our city again.

I quickly discovered that our call was just one of many calls from churches eager to help in the aftermath of the riots. The sudden outpouring of concern from churches that had no previous connection with St. Paul's overwhelmed and offended Leon and his elders. Leon told me they had scheduled a church session meeting for that night and that he would present our request, along with all the others, to his leadership team.

The next day Leon called and informed me that their session meeting had been the longest in recent memory. The room was filled with anger as they had agonized into the early hours of the morning. Why, some had asked, had so many churches that had previously seemed ignorant of St. Paul's existence decided they now ought to do something about reconciliation? Where had they been before? Why did they care now?

As I listened I had to agree that the feelings expressed by the people of St. Paul's were justified. When Leon told me they had reached a decision about their relationship with other churches, I was prepared to hear that our help would not be accepted. Instead, I learned that his session had voted to expand the partnership between St. Paul's and Brentwood. Their decision was based on two very specific factors: (1) The seeds for an ongoing relationship had already been planted by our cooperation over the years, and (2) the history of that relationship had given them reasons to expect a genuine partnership of equals, not some kind of intrusive and insensitive outside influence. They knew we cared for them and would not impose directions while ignoring what they wanted to say to us.

The relationship that was strengthened through tragedy continues to grow today. In the beginning we were just two churches meeting to talk, listen, visit each other's facilities, and share meals. More and more members of each congregation began to know members of the other by name and story. Because our joint special holiday worship services were based on these growing relationships, the services were comfortable corporate experiences. Among the traditions that grew out of these years is the practice of celebrating the Advent season together, with worship services alternating between the two churches. Other cooperative ventures, such as Vacation Bible School and after-school tutoring, have been possible because of the history of trust and care that is shared between us.

Relationships formed between persons and groups before a crisis have the best chance of weathering a crisis and being strengthened by it. Eventually, the progression of experience comes full circle. We had an opportunity to stand with St. Paul's in their hour of need, and they have been able to reciprocate. During the years of Brentwood's journey with Charles through the valley of the shadow of cancer, Leon and his people have been there for us. Charles and Leon loved and trusted each other as friends. The fact that both of them shared a calling as pastors became almost secondary.

Those of us who were tearfully present during those tender moments of our mutual relationship as churches learned some new lessons about the importance of racial reconciliation. It isn't just about resolving and healing old wounds. Authentic reconciliation simply makes it possible for people to care for each other in the deepest ways. Reconciliation allows us, in the end, to obey Jesus: "By this all men will know that you are my disciples, if you love one another" (John 13:35).

DISCOVERY AND THE SCHEDULE

CAREFUL DISCOVERY EVENTUALLY begins to affect the church's schedule. The more information that is gathered about people's available gifts and time, the more it will become clear that the church clock must be more flexible.

Many churches have recognized the need for creativity and flexibility in scheduling worship services. What if this principle were applied to the entire church calendar? What if the availability of certain gifts became a higher priority than the predetermined schedule of the church?

One of the ways to uncover insights about your church culture is to ask about the origin of the schedule:

- Why do we keep the hours we do?
- What factors went into the decision?
- Is our Sunday morning schedule still based on the idea that farmers needed time to get their morning milking and other chores done before they could get ready for church? This was a practical decision for past generations and for a different culture. Do the same conditions and factors hold true today?

I visited St. Monica's Catholic Church one evening to meet with their assimilation team (they're responsible for what they call First Contact Ministry). As I walked in I was delightfully astonished to find a receptionist and a full support-staff team serving in ministry that night! It isn't unusual that staff members support the people in ministry—but how unusual to walk into a church at 7:30 at night and find every room in the building packed with volunteers, as well as a staff on duty to meet needs! It was awesome!

What would happen if the layout, typing, and printing of your church's bulletin was done by a dedicated group of gifted people who happen to only be available at 2:00 A.M. on Thursday? God is available around the clock. No one person can keep that schedule. But together, functioning as a body, the church *can* be available any time, day or night, to meet a need.

EQUIPPING PRINCIPLES

The Launch Isn't the Voyage

Please remember that no element of the equipping process is an end in itself, but each one builds on the previous components and prepares for those that follow. Although there are certain steps that follow others on the way to becoming an equipping church, one need not conclude that one step must be complete before the next can begin. One of the crucial steps in embarking on the journey of transformation involves an assessment of every aspect of your church as it relates to the principles of equipping ministry. You will find partial examples and tentative progress in many of the components already. The way you appreciate these treasures will affect how the church responds to the changes they will face in the process of transformation.

Because the equipping church flows out of God's continual work in people's lives and in relationships, the process is never complete. The principles described in these pages will not work as a rigid program or structure imposed on a congregation. Equipping is an ongoing congregational adventure in ministry. The entire system will have to be monitored continually and occasionally evaluated thoroughly. It is a journey to be enjoyed, not a destination at which to rest.

Midcourse Corrections May Be Necessary

Speaking of journeys, repeatedly casting the vision is a critical factor in the longevity and effectiveness of the equipping model. Like continual course corrections made by an ocean liner or a rocket ship, a congregation serious about traveling in the right direction should encourage leadership to repeat, rephrase, paraphrase, and just plain keep talking about the vision in fresh and challenging ways. We forget and wander so easily! One of the powerful principles that undergirds the effectiveness of Rick Warren's Saddleback Valley Community Church is the yearly (indeed, almost monthly) cycle of recasting the vision. New people need to hear and veterans need to remember what the journey is all about.

Study Other Stories

By all means, learn from others. Find others inside as well as outside your denomination who are seeing equipping results in their churches. Particularly watch for those who are practicing what they are preaching. I am saddened when I find congregations missing out on practical help from effective and growing churches whose only "defect" is that they are part of a different denomination.

Most of the biblical principles that undergird the equipping model have no ties to any ecclesiastical model or tradition. I've had the privilege of witnessing the wonderful results of these principles in widely different churches. I've come to the conclusion that one of the first steps Christians can take in learning to practice love toward other Christians is to ask a simple question: What can we learn from these brothers and sisters?

Settle on Basics—Experiment Boldly

The process of transformation will require much trial and error. You will not discover how these principles will look in your particular situation until you make a few mistakes. Core principles within the faith measure up in the same way that G. K. Chesterton described the faith as a whole when he said, "Christianity hasn't been tried and found wanting; it has been found hard and left untried." A commitment to lay mobilization will involve a lot of hard work, but the results will be well worth it!

People Get Known through Intentional Conversations

Until we learn to value people, ministry will have limited effect. Until we take the time to discover the potential, the uniqueness, and the giftedness of people, they will remain largely unable to serve in the ways God designed them to serve.

If we wait until people share themselves with us, we will get to know only a few. Discovery affirms the idea that people get known through *intentional* conversations where we seek information that will help answer two important questions: (1) How can the rest of the church best serve this person? and (2) How can this person serve the rest of the church? This double-sided impact makes genuine discovery *holistic*. It is bigger than gift assessments, time and talent inventories, and friendly conversations. Discovery intentionally seeks to let each person in the body know they are valued as one who can be served and can serve. Discovery, like people, will always be a work in progress.

Develop a Strategy of "Planned Abandonment"

Discovery does not simply enable us to find out how people can plug into the existing church structure; sometimes, as we allow people a place and time to share their own passion, we begin to discover a gap in our own ministry that God has sent them to fill. Ministry can expand through discovery. We may well miss these golden opportunities if we define this part of the process as a means to fill slots rather than as part of God's gracious way of giving us direction.

Once a ministry has been operating for a while, the tendency is to gradually shift into a survival mode. When we do, effectiveness decreases rapidly. Ministries are not eternal commitments. Sometimes ministries must come to an end, particularly if they've served their purpose. Better a celebratory conclusion than a discouraged death from lack of interest! In the process of discovery, when we find out that the gifts needed to carry on a certain ministry no longer seem available, one thing we must consider is that, by withholding certain gifts, God is telling us that this particular ministry has served its purpose for this time and place. Leadership expert Peter Drucker has wisely pointed out that churches need to develop a strategy of "planned abandonment" of structures, programs, and methods that no longer work.

Look for the Best in the Least Likely Servants

Robert's story reminds me how easy it is to overlook the special gifts of people. When it comes to the "least," we often learn important lessons as God trains us to see the needs in others and take responsibility for meeting those needs. As we begin to do this, we are in a position to be surprised by a second series of lessons, as God shows us that those who seem most needy can also be those who give the most. The challenge for ministry leaders is to look for the best in the least likely servants.

Be Careful Not to Overlook the Obviously Gifted

Jane's story teaches me how easy it is to misjudge the obviously gifted. People who have been entrusted with significant talents, gifts, and financial resources are accustomed to being asked to do everything. They are not accustomed to having someone express a genuine interest in their needs and ask for their involvement based on a genuine understanding of them as persons. Jane's considerable gifts in ministry support were not unleashed until she began to experience directly the possibilities of what could be done a long distance from home by people at home. Once her need to understand and to be understood had been met, she became a missionary force to be reckoned with.

Show Caring before Chaos

We did not begin a relationship with St. Paul's Presbyterian Church out of a prophetic sense that there would be trouble down the road. We did it out of obedience to Christ and from an attitude of openness to opportunities. Because the groundwork of trust had been laid, the relationship was able to grow during a difficult time.

The partnerships you form with other churches may never be as severely tested as ours was, but they will allow you to expand the impact of your ministry. You and your congregation will benefit in many unforeseeable ways from relationships beyond your doors. Someday you may be the church in need!

Challenge the Schedule Idol

Church schedules often receive the treatment granted only to the documents written in stone on Mount Sinai. You would think at times that God himself dictated the hours and locations of the services in our churches. Don't be afraid to challenge the schedule idol. Once you've studied your systems and your culture, you may decide that the schedule can remain unchanged. On the other hand, as you keep on traveling in your journey to becoming an equipping church, you may begin to experience unexpected alterations in the lifestyle of the church—some of which may well involve the schedule.

EQUIPPING HEROES

St. Gerard Majella Catholic Church
Port Jefferson Station, New York
www.churchandcommunity.com/rockvillecentre/
stgerardmajella
Co-Pastor: William A. Hanson
Co-Pastor: Christopher J. Heller
Gifts Coordinator: Marie Guido

The preparation for launch and the points of growth vary in every congregation. The folks at St. Gerard Majella Catholic Church are training heroes. Through the vision of their pastors and the leadership of two innovative women, Marie Guido and Monica Harrison, St. Gerard Majella has developed one of the most biblical, creative, fun, and lively discovery seminars I've ever seen.

In response to the U.S. bishops 1992 pastoral letter, "Stewardship: A Disciple's Response," Marie and Monica and a supportive team launched two stewardship seminars. Using a clever play on words, the first seminar is called "Stewart-Ship," using the film *It's a Wonderful Life* to provoke in-depth discussions on images and attitudes that influence giving in all areas of our lives. While the first seminar focuses on time and talents, the second one is focused on how to be a responsible steward of financial resources. Through effective tracking, they provide the "invitation to continue" to all who have attended a seminar. To this end, they created a spiritual gifts assessment that responds to the language of their culture, and they developed strong systems to support the discoveries and the follow-up.

The church conducts an annual ministry fair to spur commitment of time and talent. Members of the parish see all the opportunities, supported with ministry descriptions, and then determine what their stewardship gift will be for the coming year. What is special about this community of faith is the careful (though invisible) attention to detail in their tracking, their affirmation of all those who are "working the process," the ongoing creative spirit of her leadership, and the regular sharing of stories of the life transformation that comes with being a committed steward of Jesus Christ. The impact is spreading far beyond her church walls as other parishes look to St. Gerard Majella for a vision of equipping and to observe the process that has changed the face of this parish.

QUESTIONS FOR REFLECTION AND DISCUSSION

1. Reflect back on the last two years. How often have you preached or taught on the vision and values of the equipping church?

2. Does your language reflect the biblical values and culture you are trying to sow? Make a list of some key words that could be changed and some new words that could help you picture a future equipping church.

3. How do you discover new members' "felt needs" as they join. What is the process of following up on the needs?

4. Evaluate your discovery process. Is it ongoing? Is it holistic? Is it incorporated into your church culture, and are the discoveries shared and communicated effectively?

8

Matching People with Strong Connections

> The gifts he gave were that some would be apostles, some prophets, some evangelists, some pastors and teachers, to equip the saints for the work of ministry, for building up the body of Christ, until all of us come to the *unity* of the faith and of the knowledge of the Son of God, to *maturity*, to the measure of the full *stature* of Christ.
>
> Ephesians 4:11–13 NRSV, emphasis added

CHARLES HELPED ME FOREVER by teaching me to emphasize the mind-set of abundance rather than the mind-set of scarcity. I've been amazed how often I've used terms when talking about the body of Christ that could be seen as insulting to the Lord of the church. When I limit, downsize, and "shortsight" the work of the church, I am revealing a view of Christ's body that sees too much of human frailty and not enough of Christ's sovereignty. The stories of Robert and Jane (shared in the last chapter) perfectly illustrate these lessons in the life of our church.

Everywhere I've gone I have found human frailty in churches. I've come to expect it. What continues to amaze me is what God does *in spite of* human shortcomings and failures. Look at any one of us, and even at our very best we don't have much to offer in the way of service. But bind us together under the control of the Spirit and godly leadership, and God begins to accomplish amazing things.

When Paul wrote to the Ephesians, his mental picture of their potential was nothing short of magnificent. He saw them united in faith, mature in their understanding of Christ, and genuinely living in Christlike ways.

In other words, he visualized what they could be together rather than apart. He saw them as *connected.*

The church offers one of the finest examples of the principle that the whole is more than the sum of its parts. We are much more "together in Christ" than we could ever be if we insist on seeing ourselves as loosely associated individual entities. The possibilities of what Christ can do in us and through us ought to always be open-ended.

CONNECTED VISION

IRONICALLY, THE PRINCIPLE of connections represents what can be the weakest link in the process of transformation that marks an equipping church. Time and again I've watched churches do a wonderful job gathering all the equipping components. They have taught and preached a vision, conducted culture studies, analyzed systems, and conducted extensive discovery interviews. The pieces are all in place, but the connection never takes place. The chain of change breaks just when the immovable object tremblingly starts into motion. Churches simply will not change without strong connections.

Connection happens when we take all that we've learned about the people and the needs of the church and community and begin putting them together. The process can be called "matching" or "placement." Ideally, we are, as Bruce Bugbee of Network Ministries International describes it, "placing the right people in the right places for the right reasons." When this occurs, the results transform a congregation and change lives.

Connection happens when we place the right people in the right places for the right reasons at the right time.

Connection only happens when discovery leads to follow-through. When we spend time finding out what makes people tick, and we express an interest in their interest areas, they get excited. People going through the discovery process often express the desire to become involved in some area of service. If this signal isn't picked up, the disappointment that results will make it all the more difficult to convince the person in the future that we really care about him or her. If discovery doesn't lead to real opportunity and practical follow-through, then discovery has been a waste of time.

In her book *You Can Make a Difference,* Marlene Wilson, the pioneer advocate for lay mobilization and the role of "director of volunteers," tells a story that tragically illustrates the pain that can occur when we fail to carry out this part of the process. An elderly widow had moved in with her daughter's family. Because this woman was still quite active and able to be independent, she chose to attend a church other than her daughter's. She wanted to build her own circle of friends without being a burden on her own family. A woman of faith, she planned to form a new set of relationships through her involvement in a good church.

Once she identified a church she felt comfortable in, she was intentional and systematic in immediately seeking out the membership class. But it was at this point that the church missed their first golden opportunity to minister. Why? Because there was no discovery process. This woman was never personally interviewed—by anyone. No one asked about her background with anything more than casual interest. No one inquired why she had chosen this particular church (in spite of the fact that senior citizens rarely go church shopping). And no one asked her what she was seeking through her involvement. No one asked how the church might serve her. She was welcomed with a superficial inclusion that never connected her with the body.

As part of the membership class the participants were asked to fill out a time and talent sheet that listed many opportunities for participation in the life of the church. She was handed an inventory to complete instead of being invited to participate in a caring and perceptive conversation. This widow checked almost every box with marks that practically shouted her desire to connect—somewhere, anywhere.

She eagerly awaited her chance to serve since she had checked so many boxes. Surely someone would call within a matter of days, and she would be drawn into the life of this church. She waited. She faithfully attended each week, expecting to be sought out by someone who would offer her a task she could do to participate in a meaningful way. A whole year went by without any indication that her expressed willingness to help had been noticed by anyone.

This woman was callously ignored in the one place where she should have been noticed. The very fact that she volunteered for everything should have tipped someone off that she was in need herself. This church missed a golden opportunity to make a huge difference in a person's life.

Stories like this one are all too frequent, both in large and small churches of every denomination. Too often situations like this one elicit a response such as, "Why didn't she tell someone?"—to which the only answer is, "Why didn't someone ask her?" She had come to the church for connection, healing, and community, and she thought she had said enough and left enough clues. She was a grieving widow who needed to be com-

> **No questionnaire or response card should
> ever be handed to a person to fill out unless there
> is a specific sequence of responsibility in place that
> will ensure that the information gathered will be
> used to benefit this person and the church.**

forted but in reality got little of what she needed. Where did the breakdown occur? Her church exhibited a lack of awareness of the importance of being intentional about connections. They were dabbling in the process of discovery, but it wasn't taking on a personal touch. It depended on a filled-out inventory that no one seems to have bothered to read and to formulate a response. They had no process or system in place to follow up on any of the checks the woman had made on the paper.

The discovery process requires a holistic, personal approach. A live human being needs to ask new members important questions such as, "What attracted you to our church at this time?" This single question will often provide the key response that indicates what each newcomer really needs. No questionnaire or response card should ever be handed to a person to fill out unless there is a specific sequence of responsibility in place that will ensure that the information gathered will be used to benefit this person and the church. If we don't have a process by which we can follow up, we shouldn't be asking these questions.

During the course of the eighteen months we were learning, building, and struggling before the launch of lay ministries at Brentwood, we got a precious "heads up" on the value of follow-up. Part of this awareness came from my exposure to volunteer organizations who value every single person who says they are willing to help. Unlike these nonchurch agencies, we are surrounded by potential servants. Yet the complaint I hear as much as any other in church settings is this: "We can't get anyone to help." Why? Perhaps to a large extent because we've inadvertently convinced people that they won't be valued or appreciated if they volunteer.

Thankfully we learned from our mistakes, realizing that we couldn't afford to ignore people who wanted to participate—or those who voiced a concern as well. Even a complaint can lead to an opportunity for wonderful ministry.

TASTES OF CONNECTIONS

MOST OF THE CHURCHES I visit exhibit hopeful signs of health. Even when they invite me in because they've decided they need help in the change process, I usually find that many successful efforts are already taking place. These "tastes of connection" provide people with a hint of what might result from real change. Sadly, in many cases these connections have been accidental (or, perhaps better to say, providential). After sensing a genuine need in some area of church life, someone, out of frustration or inspiration, simply took it upon themselves to do something about it. Perhaps they shared the vision with a handful of others. Eventually, that handful developed into a passionate team that made the ministry come to life. These "tastes of connection" usually lie behind the invitations we receive at Leadership Training Network.

When I arrive on the scene, I tell the story of our early days at Brentwood. My initial efforts at discovery seem trite now, but they provided us with much more information about people in our congregation (particularly new members) than we had ever had before. I instinctively knew I couldn't effectively manage or use the information by myself. So, with the help of my team, I began to create written reports for all staff members in the church. When nothing happened at the staff level, I added all the elders, deacons, and ministry leaders to those receiving updates on people I felt could find a place of service in their area of giftedness, as well as a summary of the special needs our interviews were uncovering. I was handing off people and needs to those I thought could make the best use of that information.

It didn't take long to realize we were breaking down in the connection process. Looking back, I know now that the main problem was an incomplete system. I was the steward of valuable information, but I wasn't passing it on in ways that allowed me to ensure that it was reaching the right people.

We all know what happens to "handed-off" information in church settings. If we assume that the next person to receive the information will put it to the best use, we are likely to be disappointed. Follow-up often doesn't happen, particularly when those who receive the information aren't sure it will be useful or don't take the time to invest in discovering how good the information is.

In short, our leaders were too busy leading. They didn't have time to follow up on these potential helpers. When I would ask new members and others who had expressed in the discovery process a specific interest in being involved whether they had been contacted yet, they seldom said yes. These responses revealed to me that we didn't have an effective system. It wasn't the leaders' fault. I was overloading them with information.

This breakdown eventually forced us to upgrade and complete our system. We created a liaison process, appointing "connectors" to handle information about people in our church family. I asked leaders to identify one person in their ministry area—adult ministries, Christian education, missions, youth, children, worship and music, outreach, and so on—to whom they could entrust a welcome and follow-up connection. The liaison was not the leader of or the staff member responsible for that particular ministry area. He or she was a key participant who had an interest in enlarging the ministry's effectiveness and a gift for reaching out to people. The leader of that particular ministry received a copy of the information that was given to the liaison, with the understanding that the leader was not primarily responsible for contacting the people or processing the information; we kept the ministry leaders in the information loop but rerouted the responsibility loop.

On the lay ministry team we had a liaison connections coordinator who made sure that the information about people's willingness to serve got transmitted to the liaison in the appropriate ministry area. This was the real beginning of decentralizing the process while keeping the vision and values for connecting and equipping people centralized.

CLOSING THE LOOP

AFTER CREATING THE LIAISON process, we then added a crucial next step. We closed the loop by making a point of following up on each "information handoff" to see what had been done with these people's gifts, needs, or suggestions. We began to contact each liaison within two to four weeks of a handoff to make sure that the connection had been made. These follow-up calls were not cold supervision. When there were problems, we tried to help resolve them, and we were constantly offering to help facilitate contacts with people because we knew that getting the connection made was essential to the achieving of our goal of being an equipping church.

Until we knew that the person who had expressed an interest in a certain area of ministry had in fact been contacted, we stayed involved in the process. I didn't "do" this as the director of lay ministries; I simply facilitated the process. We decentralized the connection process and immediately began to see that people were feeling more positive about the meaning of their participation. Every ministry began to take ownership in the process. They didn't have to drum up supporters on their own, but they did have to follow up on people who had already expressed an interest. There's a world of difference between making cold contacts from a membership list, hoping to stumble on a warm body to help with a ministry, and calling someone who has already let it be known they are interested in participating! It was also a huge shift from having people check a box on a time and talent sheet that ended up in a drawer somewhere to moving people from interest to involvement!

Yes, there were still special cases. The fact that we had a system actually freed us up to respond more effectively to crisis situations. If the need for ministry was immediate—health or grief situations, or other pastoral care situations—we didn't have to use the liaison system. Any of my team members who learned of the need, whether it was in a formal discovery interview or through an informal conversation, was free to take immediate action. To take an obvious example, if there was need for a pastoral call, we contacted one of the pastors with the information and then followed up with a call to the pastor within a few days to make sure that the need had been met.

This particular example illustrates an important side issue. Following up with a pastor might seem like a lack of trust, but that's not the case at all. Our pastors' plates at that time were really full, since they were still operating under the stereotypical job descriptions of pastors. It was an awkward time. Officially we had given them permission to not do everything, but experientially they still felt like (and we often still expected them to be) the "doers of all significant things."

Once we implemented the follow-up system, our pastors were relieved to know that fewer important contacts were going to be lost because someone was going to follow up within days. They realized that our checkups were valuable. They saw these follow-up contacts as a way for us to genuinely support them in their ministry.

THE CARE TEAM SUCCESS STORY

OUR CHURCH TRADITION ASSIGNS some of the work of pastoral care to the deacons. The more we realized we were asking too much of our pastors, the more we were able to encourage the deacons that their role was essential in the life of the church. Bill McNabb, our associate pastor at the time, understood the value of long-term "pastoral care" when people were facing critical situations in their lives. He knew that long-term needs often exceeded what was feasible for our pastoral staff to handle, and he recognized that the deacons' plates were full as well. An avid proponent of empowering people for ministry, and one of my mentors and greatest supporters, Bill approached me about forming a care team for the church. This "experiment" turned out to be our first real success story in the area of intentional equipping.

Bill was a gifted and passionate teacher/trainer with a heart for providing care for the short- and long-term needs in our church. He envisioned a care team made up of people with the right gifts and the right heart who would function as an authorized and recognized extension of pastoral ministries. As we discussed how to do this, it became clear that we needed two other components. First, the care team needed to be made up of people willing to commit to intense training for the ministry we would ask them to do. We wanted to go beyond affirming their obvious gifts to giving them specific support (ministry equipment) in order to help them succeed in their calling. (In the next chapter I'll discuss the importance of training.) Second, by giving them training and skill sets appropriate to their calling, the church could commission (and value) them as the channels of pastoral care. They were not to be the substitute team who stepped in because the real team (the pastors) couldn't be there. We wanted to agree and affirm that their ministry *was* the real thing. We wanted them to accept our acceptance of the fact that when they stepped into a crisis situation or responded to a particular need, by God's grace they were as good as it gets for that moment.

Bill and I began to identify the people in our congregation who fit the profile we had developed for the care team. Other church members had helped us brainstorm the profile, answering the question, "What are the gifts, the criteria, and the talents needed for this care team ministry?" Then we began a prayerful process of matching. Our system of discovery interviews and tracking was at the point where we were able to clearly identify twelve people who would be ideal partners in our inaugural care team. We agreed that this was the right number to help us measure the effectiveness of the experiment.

The people who made up the original care team were certainly unique, but they shared some common gifts. The strongest gift represented was mercy. These were people who could listen. They had a way of being there in the middle of a crisis or need and making a difference by their presence, even more than by what they said. These were people who already had a reputation for caring. Among the care team members were also several who had been deeply touched by others in a time of need and were thus open to ministering to others who needed someone to come alongside.

MAKING THE CALLS

ONCE WE IDENTIFIED OUR dream team, we made phone calls to invite each person into this specific ministry. I will never forget those conversations. They provided rich and memorable moments for me. In one sense, it felt like a setup. We were calling to offer them the opportunity to do what we already knew they really wanted to do!

Each of the people I had the privilege of calling were so thankful to be asked. I cherish one of those calls in particular. Bill is one of God's special treasures! He is still actively involved today—in his late eight-ies. I called Bill and described the ministry to him. I briefly shared the vision of a care team in our church to serve as an extension of the pastoral ministry. Then I told him that Bill McNabb and I believed he had the right heart and the depth of understanding required for this ministry. We really wanted him to be on this care team.

I will never forget his answer. Bill had suffered a heart attack not long before I called him. He said, "I told God, 'If you let me live, I will make my life count for you.'" Bill had already made his life count. But when he joined the care team, he did so with reckless abandon. He was like a kid playing in a new sandbox—but the sandbox was caring ministries! Fifteen years later he is still a key leader in our church's caregiving ministries. In him we found a man who had the right gifts and a heart filled with passion to meet the needs of others in the way he had had his own needs met. He felt (and still feels) that God allowed him to survive his heart attack so that he could care for other people. Bill has taken full advantage of God's generosity, and countless hurting people have benefited.

TRAINING COURSE

THE ORIGINAL CARE TEAM began with a ten-week training course in which we met each week with Bill McNabb. We learned and practiced listening skills, and we discussed how to pray and how to be present and helpful without drawing attention to ourselves. We learned how not to think of ourselves as rescuers—how important it was to listen but not take responsibility for solving the problem. We participated in exercises designed to help us deal with our own mortality; to that end we wrote our own obituaries so we could understand better what it feels like to face death. One memorable (and revealing) exercise Bill led us through involved deciding what would be the last five possessions we would give away. We read and discussed Elisabeth Kübler-Ross's book *On Death and Dying*. Bill invited a grief counselor to help us appreciate what goes into listening with care to a grieving person. We had a session with a clinical psychologist who talked about suicide, with a particular emphasis on knowing when to refer someone to a professional counselor. The training had a definite impact on us as a team—and it surely affected the level of care that people received on an ongoing basis. My experience with "Joe" (I shared his story in the introduction to this book) occurred during my term on the care team. I had originally decided to go through the training with the care team in order to become a trainer, but the direct participation in caring ministries met a deep longing in my soul. I loved the authentic, heartfelt connections.

As a result of our success with the care team, we added Stephen Ministries to our ministry options and spread out the responsibility for pastoral care even more. Bill McNabb launched and nurtured the value of connectional caregiving by the people of the church. Through the care team and the intentional equipping of laypeople for pastoral care, Bill helped break the old paradigm that only pastors are to tend to the needy. Our capacity to respond effectively to short-term and long-term care needs expanded measurably. Care team involvement where there was a death in the family lasted at least a year, as team members made a point of remembering birthdays, anniversaries, and holidays, helping the grief process to move along in healthy ways. More and more folks within our congregation were experiencing the joys of ministry. We were growing toward life as a real and dynamic body.

> **Through the care team and the intentional equipping of laypeople for pastoral care, Bill helped break the old paradigm that only pastors are to tend to the needy.**

Much of this happened as a result of what seemed to be "accidental" circumstances but were really providential connections. God was guiding us. All of this flowed from the simple effort to do what Jesus did, namely, to care for people.

What if more connections within the body of Christ were intentional? What would happen if more people were matched with opportunities that best suited them? Great things could be accomplished for Christ!

WORSHIP, PLUS TWO

ONE OF THE PUBLIC evidences of the underlying value we place on connections has come to be known as "Worship, Plus Two." We will always maintain the central role of worship in our life as a church. Our first point of connection flows from our worshiping God together. Because we are co-heirs with Christ of God's gracious gifts (Romans 8:17), we also have a share in each other. The "plus two" represents our acknowledgement that there is a time to serve and a time to be served—a time to give and a time to receive and be nurtured in the body of Christ. This has been one of the strongest messages we communicate in our new-member classes. We don't just tell them that we expect them to participate by serving. We also tell them we expect them to open themselves up when they need serving. We want to create an atmosphere where people understand that depending on others will eventually be part of their experience—if it hasn't been already. And we want them to know that, when they refuse to look at their dependence as a failure, it can be a good part of their experience of God's grace. Nurture is an important element in our spiritual growth, as is service. We value being a connectional church, and we suggest *two* connections, namely, nurture and service.

Charles once used a powerful illustration that helped me understand the principle of "seasons of service" in my life as a believer. Recurring health challenges have sometimes made it impossible for me to participate in the ways I've desperately wanted to. Many times over the years he reminded our congregation of this truth:

> There are times when we as Christians need to carry the stretcher.
> There are other times when we need to walk alongside the stretcher.
> And, whether we like it or not, there are times when we need to be
> on the stretcher, being carried by others.

This imagery helped me immeasurably when jaw surgeries left me helpless and silent—unable to even say thanks to those who were carrying me during that part of the journey.

We give our new members specific instructions about responding to opportunities for service. Please tell us, we say, if the invitation comes at the wrong time. We give them permission, even after they've expressed an interest in or passion for some area of ministry, to decide that it is not the right season in their life for that particular opportunity. But the underlying emphasis is always on connection. Our approach interprets *serving* and *being served* as the two-way link that creates connection. The end result is connection—strong ligaments linking the parts of the body—and not just service. We believe that this emphasis has made us unique as a church. Our public acknowledgment that we count it as high an honor to be served as to serve has nurtured bonds of mutual reliance that really are bodylike in their effects. As a church we function in the middle of one of the largest and most depersonalized metropolitan areas in the world. People naturally assume that family life and social cohesiveness is nonexistent in Los Angeles. Yet we are a connectional church that thrives on connections. We foster them, strengthen them, and celebrate them every chance we get. The strength of these connections can be seen in the way our congregation reaches out to the world. Whether we are serving one another or joyfully representing Christ in service in places throughout the world, our connections back to Brentwood and in and through Christ keep us alive!

INDIVIDUAL CONNECTIONS

A GOOD CONNECTION MATCHES a person with a particular need. That person represents a set of gifts, talents, availability, and experience. The connection may place the person into a large working group or program, or even into the church as a whole. Many, however, will be individual, person-to-person connections.

Connections take the title of "minister" and apply it to people who usually hear themselves called "laity" or "volunteers." Their gifts and abilities gain value in the process as they become more likely to respond to needs that come to them along the way. But the two-way street of giving and receiving is always open for traffic. I've seen this principle work in countless situations. When we connect people with mission opportunities, such as working among orphans employed in a Mexico landfill or helping to build a Habitat home, those who serve on those projects are changed. Even though they provide real help, they are overwhelmed by the need and discouraged by the seeming insignificance of what they can genuinely accomplish. Their hearts are broken. Others on the team must gather around and affirm their grief. It is never a bad thing to let our hearts be broken by the things that break God's heart. But when the breaking takes place, we need the support of our brothers and sisters in Christ.

The line between giving and receiving is very thin, and I think this truth is at least part of what lies behind Jesus' statement, "It is more blessed to give than to receive" (Acts 20:35). Perhaps Saint Francis of Assisi gave the best one-line explanation of Jesus' words—"For it is in giving that we receive."

The power of connections in the church has an impact on how people view their own value. But connections do not bestow value on people. Authentic connections recognize the value that is already present in a person because he or she is created in God's image, has been saved by grace, and has been uniquely gifted to participate in the life of the body of Christ. Gifts and talents are sometimes-hidden evidences of value. God allows believers to help one another discover, receive training for, and exercise these evidences of value.

CONNECTING BEYOND THE WALLS

A GENUINE APPRECIATION OF the variety and quantity of gifts available in a church will eventually lead to the conclusion that the opportunities to exercise these gifts within the church walls will quickly be exhausted. Besides, God has called many of his people to be active in service in the

> **It is never a bad thing to let our hearts be broken by the things that break God's heart. But when the breaking takes place, we need the support of our brothers and sisters in Christ.**

world. Individual gifts of evangelism, as well as the universal commission given all believers to share their faith, make it important for those involved in facilitating connections to see the church walls as porous rather than solid.

Even in very active churches the amount of time people spend inside the walls of the church will be small compared to the time spent out in the world. The kind of service to which God calls us cannot be limited by structures. The great commandment to love our neighbor includes the possibility that our neighbor may someday become our brother or sister in the faith. Service is not limited to that end, but certainly includes that possibility among its objectives.

During the process of discovery, most churches will find that their influence already extends beyond their walls. Discovery will not be complete without questions like:

- Who is already serving in nonchurch volunteer agencies?
- In what ways are we actively teaching people to view their lives beyond the walls of the church as places that hold opportunities for service?
- In what ways are we affirming and celebrating the ministries of our people beyond the church walls?
- What relationships are we establishing with other churches in our area? If our community experienced some kind of disaster, how would we join other Christians and people of faith in responding?
- What relationships are we building with other nonprofit organizations in the area so that when we find a person in our church who has a passion for another organization's mission, we can bring the two together? (Some kind of ongoing follow-up system is vital when these connections are made.)

If you are a pastor, you may now be muttering under your breath, "I have enough trouble just getting Sunday school teachers. I can't send people to minister outside the church, too!" There's something right and captivating about the biblical images of the church in action, but perhaps you're having a hard time seeing it where you are. "It's okay," you admit, "for big churches to put up low-income housing and start nonprofit corporations, but we're just a small church and we don't have that kind of money."

If this is what you're thinking, let me tell you something that may seem funny. This has less to do with money and more to do with a mind-set about God. Is there a difference between a church with a budget of $60,000 that struggles with $100,000 dreams and a church with a $2 million budget talking about $3 million dreams? Not really! I've sat in meetings in both of these types of churches (and a lot of churches in-between) and heard nearly identical phrases spoken at all of them. My favorite is, "We just don't have that kind of money!"

You see, it really is a mind-set about God, and it's called the mind-set of scarcity. It's the "we don't have it, so we can't be expected to do it" thinking. I know about this because I've struggled with it a lot! The mind-set of scarcity short-circuits creative thinking, lets us off the hook too easily, or sometimes even puts us on the wrong hook.

To put this in perspective, if money were no issue, what would you do? I've discovered that behind the mind-set of scarcity often lies a fear that can be expressed this way: "I'm sure relieved we don't have the means to do this, because if we did, I'd have to admit that I don't have a clue about how to do it!" The mind-set of scarcity applies to abilities as well as to funds, which is why in the end I call it a mind-set about God. I have to keep reminding myself of one of those time-worn but tested rules: Where God guides, he provides. God may not always provide in the way we expect, but we really ought to have an attitude that leaves God plenty of room to operate, and perhaps even to work a miracle or two!

Sound familiar? These are just a few of the "yeah, buts" I've encountered when folks begin to discuss ways of serving in the community. They are certainly the kinds of objections a pastor has to settle in his or her mind during the movement toward gift-based ministry in a church. The responses to these objections will profoundly affect the job description and expectations of the director of equipping ministries.

At Leadership Training Network we have come to believe that a church that has fully mobilized her people will generally see a fifty-fifty breakdown, where half the people function inside the church walls while

---

A church that has fully mobilized her people will generally see a fifty-fifty breakdown, where half the people function inside the church walls while half function outside in the community.

half function outside in the community. When it comes to places of service, God surely wants his people spreading out and salting the world. We are to be light—a light that is meant to go places, a light that is to invade the darkness of the world.

Those who serve as directors of equipping ministries or director of lay mobilization function best with the widest field of opportunities. Their job is to channel the right people to the right places based on need, passions, and gifts—not on whether the ministry is inside the walls of the church. The impact on our communities that results from committed Christians infiltrating the social sector by living out their faith through service as they model Christ's love in all they do—whether building houses, serving in soup kitchens, tutoring, or helping the homeless with résumés and job placement—will change lives. It is the finest evangelism tool we have.

BIG HURDLES

WHY ARE THESE THINGS so difficult to do? I think part of the problem is the fact that we find it easier to *talk* about gift-based ministry than to commit ourselves to the trials and tribulations of applying this value to the way we actually do things. In a local church, the commitment starts with the senior pastor. Senior pastors cannot be those who think they can do everything but are willing to let a few people help them. Rather, they are those who know they can't do everything, don't want to do everything, and are not willing to do everything; they welcome others to come alongside with their gifts in order to form a powerful team for Christ.

Another hurdle is the failure to remember that the largest group of people available and equipped to help in any ministry will not volunteer to do so on their own. They have to be detected and identified as passionate or gifted and then invited to respond to a specific opportunity to serve.

My favorite senior citizen in our church (who prefers to be known as "chronologically gifted") taught me an extraordinary lesson about the importance of intentional connections. Russell had been an elder for many years, functioning in various capacities. Not only was he an effective mentor (especially to me), he also spent hours serving and encouraging those he was called to lead. He was the elder responsible for lay ministries at a time when my team was hosting a training on "How to Invite People into Ministry." I was facilitating the training, and I had just asked the group where they felt the responsibility of "initiation" for the connection should be—with the leaders of the church or with those who were volunteering. One of the participants expressed her frustration about the fact that people were waiting to be asked to serve. She felt that, because we had done so much work creating ministry opportunities and promoting them through several channels, the people should be more proactive and just step up and serve where there was a need.

In the middle of this conversation, Russell raised his hand. A wise smile cracked his "eighty-something"-year-old face as he said, "I've never volunteered for anything in my life!" I was stunned. Russell did everything around our church. How could he not have volunteered? At a worship service a few weeks before, we had celebrated his fifty-five years of service for the Boy Scouts of America. The room became very quiet. At first we thought he was joking, but it became apparent that he was dead serious. I broke the silence and asked if he was willing to share why he had never volunteered to serve. His simple yet profound words provided one of the most potent lessons I've learned in ministry. Russell replied, "I just figured if I was needed or if my gifts were of value, they would ask me."

Most people are like Russell. If asked wisely, they would be glad to help, especially the "chronologically gifted." Many seniors are reluctant to take the bold step to offer their gifts, but they almost always say yes when invited into the party. People who like to do odd or rare kinds of work often cannot believe that the whole world isn't competing along with them for the opportunity. Jesus called twelve disciples, but only one of them was an accountant. Matthew's Gospel displays the attention to detail of a mind focused on order and tracking. While Matthew stayed in the background throughout the ministry of Jesus and the others, he surely kept good notes.

To use David's phrase in Psalm 139, people are "fearfully and wonderfully made." If we can identify some of the uniqueness with which God has gifted them for service, and then ask them to put these gifts to use, we will have released a powerful force for good and for God in the world.

Team-based ministry pursues with passion the principle that while gifts are given to individuals, they are given for a corporate purpose.

Gift-based ministry seeks a continual state of alertness and awe with respect to God's marvelous plan. Team-based ministry pursues with passion the principle that while gifts are given to individuals, they are given for a corporate purpose. Gifts reach their maximum value and are put to their best use when they function in unity. This is too important a principle to leave the practice of gifts to accidental connection or to a small percentage of impulsive volunteers.

Charles set a powerful example for all of us of servant leadership. He defined his own success by how well the rest of us saw ourselves as ministers and then acted as ministers. He was once asked to share the most significant word of advice he could pass on to other pastors. This was his response:

> I would ask them to not see their job as running the church, but as empowering the people of God to be the ministers they are called to be. Leaders come and go, but there will always be a body of people, and they need to claim the ministry God has given them. Recognizing this makes me feel totally different internally. I take my reward in seeing the payoff through people living out their gifts.

There's an interesting biblical application about connection that comes from Paul's letter to the Ephesians, which we are highlighting throughout this book: "From him the whole body, joined and held together by every supporting ligament, grows and builds itself up in love, as each part does its work" (4:16). The parts (people) of the body of Christ are "joined and held together" by ligaments, that is, by connections. These connections represent the fact that we need each other and we need what we can do for each other. The equipping church devotes itself to the ongoing task of connecting people to points of service and to each other.

EQUIPPING PRINCIPLES

Intentionality Doesn't Guarantee Infallibility

The ministry of connecting people with points of service will never be an exact science. At Brentwood we are getting better at it, but we're still learning. The increased value of effectively identifying people's gifts and placing them in the most appropriate ministries has led to a continual development of tools. We now have a wide selection of methods to help people discover their giftedness. But unless we are clear about our goals and committed to using the information wisely once we get it, all we will have accomplished is to gather vast amounts of data.

We need to demonstrate to people that the information they entrust to us will be used to establish them in places where God can use them. We also need to remind them that if the "fit" isn't right, we want to know about it right away. To do so tells them we are doing our best, but we are not assuming that we are infallible!

A Senior Advocate Is Required

In addition to preaching, teaching, casting (and recasting) the vision, and modeling shared ministry, the pastor's role is one of advocate. Any radical changes in the way you do things will require an advocate. The church always has been (and I fear always will be) resistant to change. If the values are clear and all agree what the path is, you march hand in hand toward that goal. However, the reality is that not everyone chooses to join the march at the same time (or at all).

At Brentwood we established the values for what the new culture would be, and in addition to our "launch," we began to define who we were in the context of our new-member classes. We were uncompromisingly clear about the covenant of membership and our value for "Worship, Plus Two" namely, that each person is gifted and called to be in ministry. We were also quick to add clarifiers. My own journey compelled me to remind folks that there were "seasons of service" and that while we believed that their faith commitment compelled them to serve, it needed to be at the right time and in the right place. Additionally we wanted them to be in a God-honoring ministry where they served out of their giftedness and not merely out of obligation. We told every new person how important the yes is and, equally as crucial, how to say no when the circumstances dictated it. We also noted that if anyone found himself or herself in a place in ministry that simply was not the right fit, to let us know and we would do all we could to remedy the situation or redirect the placement.

Wouldn't you know it! Sure as you proclaim a value, someone will call you on it! A gentleman (new to Brentwood but not new to church involvement) came to my office one day and told me he recognized he was in the wrong ministry. After several months of trying to make it work, he realized he had said yes without recognizing how far out of his area of giftedness, time availability, and comfort zone his role took him. He reminded me of my promise in the new-member class to try to get the best "fit" for all. He offered to stay in the ministry until we found a replacement and even agreed to train his successor. I thanked him for his honesty and his willingness to keep serving until we found another person, and I assured him we would find the right person for the role. I also asked him if he had talked this through with his ministry leader. He said he had, and that she had assured him he would grow to like his ministry!

This was early in my service as director of lay ministries. Many church members at that point still didn't trust the role and the process, and they simply liked church just fine the old way, thank you very much. When the ministry leader found out I had agreed to replace this person, she was furious and went immediately to Charles to complain. He called me and with a bit of humor in his voice said, "I hear we have a bit of a problem." He asked me what had gone on, and I laid it out for him, step by step. He then asked me what I intended to do about it. I responded by asking him, "What would you have had me do differently, and did we live into our new values?" In reply he said that he was convinced we had indeed lived into our stated values and that I had handled it just right. I then asked another question: "What are *you* going to do about it?" Please note that I did not ask this question in sarcasm or jest. We were both very aware that this was the first challenge to our new ministry mindset. If the senior pastor had not advocated for the new way of "doing church" and for the new values, lay ministries would be dead in the water. He took this role very seriously, and because he did, we were able to bring the reluctant leaders along. He advocated for the biblical vision and the church-established values and challenged the leaders to "live in the tension" of the transition.

Handoffs Require Follow-up

Our biggest lessons were learned through mistakes. We rarely got things right the first time. We got so excited about discovery and the idea of matching people's gifts with the needs that we overlooked some crucial factors.

One significant mistake we made was assuming that matching a gift and talent with a certain need took care of most of the important questions. We had to learn that any handoff of an assignment or person had to be done with the understanding that follow-up would take place. We learned to make an intentional and concerted effort to make sure queries, offers of help, and specific assignments were followed up on. Yes, it took time. It required explanations at times. But we became convinced, because of what we learned through our failures, that closing the loop was an excellent way to demonstrate that we were serious about our stewardship of people.

Appoint Ministry Connectors

I remember visiting one large, successful church that was going through what they described as "growing pains." They invited me to help them evaluate their system. The pastor, a dynamic leader, was a reluctant participant in the process, and he was frustrated because he couldn't put his finger on what was going wrong. They were doing many things right. Their discovery work was first-rate. Yet, as the staff described their efforts to me, I could see the pastor's level of frustration rising.

I came to see that they had overlooked the principle of connections. They had no way of really knowing if the practical information they were generating about the people in the congregation was actually being used. I finally said, "You've done a great job in bringing all the parts of an effective system together. You have the body, with all of its various components, spread out on the operating room table. What I don't see are any ligaments. How are these things connected, and how do you make sure they're connected?"

In a flash of insight the pastor bolted upright. "That's it! That's what we're missing! How do we create ligaments?" He saw the light! Bless him.

Ligaments are connections. Ephesians 4:16 says, "From him [Christ] the whole body, joined and held together by every supporting ligament, grows and builds itself up in love, as each part does its work." At Brentwood we appointed liaisons (connectors) in each of our ministry areas to make sure that we had ligaments. We had specific training for all who served as liaisons, because we wanted them to understand how significant their role was in the overall well-being of the church.

The larger the church, the more crucial it becomes to make the ligaments personal and effective. It is literally a critical link in the system. Without oversight throughout the process, you will not be able to note where problems are and then correct them. People will get lost and discouraged, even though you have an otherwise well-designed system.

Appreciate What Has Gone Before

This principle fits snugly next to other parts of the equipping model and shows up often during our exploration of the culture and systems in a local church. Healthy transformation will not happen without an appreciation of what has gone before. Those who are already serving in places that provide the right fit for their gifts and talents should not be made to feel that all the talk about change means they will have to do something else. Instead, they can serve as "seed examples" of the way equipping ought to work for everyone within the church—connecting people with a place of ministry that really fits them.

Anytime you can use stories from your own church to illustrate the components of the equipping model, you validate what God is already doing and build on what is already familiar to your particular church. Insight into the culture and the systems often come from looking at what is already working. Invariably, these are the places where connection has already occurred.

Take Seriously the Stewardship of Time

One of the key decisions that guided Brentwood through the process of transformation was to take seriously the stewardship of time. When we talked about and planned for greater involvement by the majority of our church membership, we kept reminding ourselves that we did not just want to get more people busy; we wanted them to be doing what God designed them to do.

We have come to understand that when we show we care about the way people invest their time by the way we connect them to ministry, the people themselves feel valued. If their ministry is worthwhile and the time they invest is worthwhile, then their sense of participation and contribution rises. They discover that they really do have something to offer that makes a difference among God's people.

Porous Walls Should Exist between the Church and World

When we speak about porous church walls, we are emphasizing the continuity of ministry opportunities that ebb and flow from inside the church out into the world. We recognize the significance of seeing the church as a place of safety. The need for balance creates tension. How can we preserve the church as a genuine place of security for lost people while not creating such a safe and secure place that no one can get in!

When we talk about how ministry can be received, the church ought to picture herself with doors swinging inward for the world. When we talk about how ministry can be exercised, the church ought to picture herself with doors swinging outward into the world.

The church walls are not large enough to contain all the gifts that God has given to the congregation. Ministry will leak out. Gifts will escape. Service will impact the world. If the gospel is true, "leaking out" is definitely part of the plan and the message!

EQUIPPING HEROES

Church of the Resurrection
Leawood, Kansas
www.cor.org
Senior Pastor: Adam Hamilton
Director of Lay Ministries: Gia Garey

Some churches have a way of inspiring a visitor with their vision before they even put it into words. The facilities, decor, imagery, and kind of welcome speak volumes to a newcomer. Church of the Resurrection (COR), just outside Kansas City, Missouri, is one such church. They have put visuals to their vision. When a new person walks through the door, it doesn't take long to figure out where they belong—and that they are expected to grow. Why? Because, at COR, everyone is encouraged to head for the summit!

Director of lay ministries Gia Garey is responsible for the Summit Stewardship trail, and she and her team assist members in mapping their service path. Recognizing that life's spiritual journey is like climbing a mountain, Church of the Resurrection uses the metaphor of the summit in all that they do. COR is very intentional about providing opportunities for spiritual growth. They begin by inviting people to journey on three different trails: the Spiritual Strength and Endurance trail (discipleship), the Summit Stewardship trail (service), and the Valley Ministry trail (evangelism and missions). Each trail has a director who guides the traveler as he or she journeys to the summit. (See the brief profile of COR in chapter 10.)

The lay ministry team has done the hard work over the years, laying the foundational systems for the discovery, the connections and the follow-up process. Meanwhile their senior pastor, Adam Hamilton, has continually given voice to the equipping values through preaching. Everyone receives a variety of opportunities to gain understanding and to connect with the rest of the congregation. The shared vision energizes this church!

The church produces a booklet (updated annually for the September "base camp") that maps out all service opportunities. Each new year church members participate in the discovery of ministry opportunities. After attending a spiritual gifts discovery class, each member will meet with a trained interview team one-on-one for approximately an hour to tell his or her story and receive guidance on which path to begin taking. Each handoff is an intentional process based on readiness. An "action form" is either e-mailed or sent to the ministry leaders and also retained by the interviewer.

Interviewers follow up both with the ministry leaders and the individual to see if there has been a connection and to discern if the needs are being met.

Leaders make a follow-up call at the three-month point to see if the ministry is a good fit and to determine if those who serve are receiving the training they need to be successful in their ministry. A final follow-up is made after one year has passed in order to assess the member's service and to determine if he or she is growing. Gia reminded me that "the primary concern is spiritual growth; that's what all of this is about." During this time the team is always looking for potential new leaders, and when discovered, they are directed toward the church's UpWord Bound University for extensive training in leadership development.

The team has built information systems as a way of capturing information about an individual's gifts, passions, interview information, ministry placement, evaluation of placement, leadership development involvement, and recognition. But COR did not become a lively organism overnight. It took two years to prepare the soil and build an infrastructure for discovery and the follow-up process so that they could live into the values of the "summit" program. According to Gia, "It will always be a work in progress." The process is always fluid in order to respond to the growth and restructuring that comes with increasing numbers of people and ministries.

The church's high value on excellence creates a climate of ongoing change and adaptability. What is unique about COR's model is the collaborative vision of three staff directors who oversee the three paths that can be traveled by an individual as they journey toward full maturity.

> First Baptist Church of Leesburg
> Leesburg, Florida
> www.fbcleesburg.org
> Senior Pastor: Charles Roesel

This church impacts the community with the motto "Meeting People—Sharing Christ." A member testifies that the church was always there for him, even when he wasn't ready for the "church." Eager to be an authentic model of community connections, First Baptist Church of Leesburg sees needs and finds ways to meet them. This church is a pioneer in "ministry evangelism" in the community and has launched many 501(c)(3) nonprofit agencies, often in collaboration with other organizations that were already involved in or had a heart for the presenting need. A few examples:

- Charity School: a "Saturday" Sunday school where inner-city kids are invited to be picked up by a bus and to play and to be taught from the Bible. As facilities began to be taxed, and ministry leaders found areas they were not reaching, they created the RIOT (Righteous Invasion of Truth) Bus—a bright-orange bus that is a portable, mobile sidewalk Sunday school with a platform that drops down and speakers that pop up so three to four hundred kids a week can be reached with music and Sunday school activities in their neighborhoods.

- Alpha-Omega: a public school program providing before- and after-school day care at a rate greatly reduced from traditional day care centers.

- Day Spring Ministries: a fine-arts ministry providing piano lessons; instrument lessons; dance, singing, and drama opportunities; and even a dinner theater. They have been surprised by its success in reaching people who weren't being reached in other ways.

- Bryce's Pregnancy Care Center: a ministry created to address the large number of teen pregnancies by offering an alternative to abortion. Team members teach Lamaze classes, as well as classes on nutrition and safe sex. It is the only such center serving several counties. First Baptist Church's administrative pastor Art Ayris states that even though this pregnancy care center is tied to a national organization, "they are making a difference on a local level, demonstrating that you change the world one person at a time."

More than sixty ministries, both inside and outside the church walls, make an impact in their community. More are being developed, including a proposed Christian high school. First Baptist of Leesburg does not do it alone. They collaborate at every level, including seeking grant monies for funding. They see needs and meet them. As Art Ayris says, "It's almost like the movie *Field of Dreams:* 'Build it, and they will come.' The process is to listen to what God is telling us. We pray. We fast. We seek the Lord. We look at what the needs of the community are, and as we start with each particular need, God provides the people. The key to our philosophy is to begin right where you are, use what you've got, and begin ministering in that situation."[1]

---

[1]Excerpts taken from an interview with Dave Travis of Leadership Network. The complete text can be found in Eureka, the information database of Leadership Network.

QUESTIONS FOR REFLECTION AND DISCUSSION

1. In what ways do you value the ministry carried out by those who serve in agencies beyond the walls of the church?

2. How do you connect ministry opportunities with people who check a box on a time and talent sheet or express an interest during the discovery process in serving?

3. Are there any missing ligaments in your systems?

4. How are you equipping people to be the hands and feet of pastoral care? How are you communicating and embodying this value to the congregation?

5. If you are the director of equipping ministry, what systems have you established to develop relationships with community organizations that would enable you to place people in service opportunities in their ministry or organization?

9

Pushing Back a Little

> It was he who gave some to be apostles, some to be prophets, some to be evangelists, and some to be pastors and teachers, to *prepare God's people* for works of service, so that the body of Christ may be built up until we all reach unity in the faith and in the knowledge of the Son of God and become mature, attaining to the whole measure of the fullness of Christ.
>
> Ephesians 4:11–13, emphasis added

As IMPORTANT AS PREACHING about service is, it usually doesn't get people involved in service. As valuable as teaching about service is, it rarely moves people to actively serve. Commanding people to serve often creates little more than echoes. Begging people to serve doesn't have much effect either. People must be trained or, to use Paul's word to the Ephesians, *prepared* to serve.

The fact that people know their gifts and talents doesn't necessarily mean that they understand how and where to apply those gifts. They need help, and they will benefit from living models. They are more likely to overcome discouragement if they know someone cares about their involvement and success.

In Paul's vision of what the church should look like, he included the bridge of preparation between the gifted leadership on one shore and the purpose of a mature body of Christ on the other. God has chosen to grow the body of Christ through human leaders. The responsibilities are both specific and sobering. The four stated ultimate objectives (unity in the faith, unity in the knowledge of the Son of God, maturity, and attaining **149** to the whole measure of the fullness of Christ) all depend on the faithfulness of those God has gifted to lead the church.

Ponder this: Would it not create a significant change in the way church leaders do ministry if they all committed to evaluate their effectiveness based on the degree to which they are preparing others to do ministry?

THE EQUIPPING VISION

WHEN I BECAME THE DIRECTOR of lay ministries at Brentwood, I soon realized that I needed training, and very little, if any, was available in church circles for the work I had been called to do. My discovery of Directors of Volunteers in Agencies (DOVIA) and other nonprofit organizations offered me invaluable assistance in finding my way in a new world.

My experiences with those organizations led to a startling and disturbing realization. The church is one of the few, if not the only, nonprofit organization that does not require training for service in leadership. Churches tend to assume that people of faith will automatically have the kind of commitment, skill, and experience to carry out whatever is asked of them. If the church gets someone to say yes to a role, there will more likely be a sigh of relief than some specific guidelines about what the job requires. The how-tos are often shockingly overlooked.

The church is one of the few, if not the only, nonprofit organization that does not require training for service in leadership. Churches tend to assume that people of faith will automatically have the kind of commitment, skill, and experience to carry out whatever is asked of them.

The citywide soccer league in our town recruits a large number of parents to serve as coaches and assistants. I recently talked to one father who had to give up his role as an assistant coach because he could no longer commit to the amount of time for training and certification that the role demanded of him. His job as an assistant coach required much more training than a typical elder or deacon can expect to receive from a church. How can we describe a role as an "important ministry" when we expect people to do it without any preparation?

During one of the earthquakes that are part of life in our Southern California community, a doctor from our church heard that a nearby hospital was in need of assistance. He went to volunteer, but they had to decline his offer. The problem had nothing to do with his medical qualifications. He simply had not been trained by the Red Cross and was therefore ineligible to offer his considerable abilities. As shortsighted as we might think this policy is, it does point out the seriousness of the issue of qualification. Why shouldn't we care as deeply about the preparation of those who are dealing with matters of the soul?

Let me quickly add that training and certifications are not a *substitute* for giftedness and talent, but they definitely work together. Good preparation improves morale and strengthens connections and greatly increases the possibility of long-term, effective ministry.

Before we look more carefully at the nature of preparation, we must face another barrier that often derails lay mobilization.

THE VISION CONFRONTS STEREOTYPES

EVERY PASTOR I'VE INTERVIEWED has a list of classic volunteer disappointments. These are the stories that usually lurk beneath a pastor's reluctance to get behind lay mobilization. Brad Smith calls these the "Hall of Fame of Volunteer Failures":

- key people who energetically volunteered to do a big task, then never finished it
- volunteers who didn't show up as promised, leaving paid staff members to pick up the pieces
- committee members who lacked faith and said no to everything
- committee members who were overcontrolling in their oversight assignments
- volunteers who became possessive and exclusionary in their roles
- the volunteer board that overturned the staff's five-month planning and research activities with a five-minute discussion and decision

These painful experiences do increase the difficulty of gaining broad approval for lay mobilization. Unless these memories are handled carefully and deliberately, they can create false stereotypes and negative expectations that will undermine efforts to entrust volunteers with ministry.

Yet, if truth be told, I've also seen the other side of the picture. Volunteers have their own list of grievances about their participation in the work of the church. We might call these the "Hall of Fame of Mobilization Failures":

- Volunteers come with ideas to share about the ministry but are never given an opportunity to speak.
- Volunteers have a significant amount of knowledge and experience in the area in which they've offered to help, but they are treated as though they know nothing.

- Volunteers come with the expectation that they are to assist a leader and discover they have been put in charge.
- Volunteers continually feel as though responsibilities are delegated without regard for training, orientation, or experience.
- Volunteers offer to help and never receive an opportunity.

The responsibility for improvement rests on both sides, but leaders must lead.

One of the sure signs of unresolved trust appears when staff members delegate a task to a lay leader and then later reassert control. Another occurs when a planning meeting is convened, and the volunteers discover that the plans have already been finalized and that their presence at the meeting is only required for simple job assignments. They came to contribute ideas and help shape the plan. Instead, they are just issued marching orders. A message of disrespect and lack of significance gets communicated. People quickly conclude that they are little more than gofers for the staff. The effects can be deadly. Why should people who donate their time take personal ownership and invest in efforts that may be taken from them at a moment's notice? Sadly, a resulting reluctance to serve and a seeming lack of commitment on the part of volunteers simply reinforce negative stereotypes, and the cycle of distrust and failures leads to an atmosphere in which the idea of laypeople participating dynamically in ministry becomes a less-than-cherished ideal.

Intentional effort must be made to break the cycle of low expectations. When people know that paid staff members believe they will succeed, and when they know that their efforts will be respected, they will not only accomplish wonderful things, but they will also grow into effective ministers within the areas of their gifts and talents. What kind of intentional effort am I talking about? Brad Smith puts it well: "The best way to deal with 'team ministry hesitation' is to get it out in the open and talk about what can be done to build better systems and to build mutual trust between paid staff and nonpaid staff." In other words, the lack of trust needs to be named before it can be confronted and subsequently eliminated.

PUSH BACK A LITTLE

THE DISCUSSIONS, AND PERHAPS ARGUMENTS, that must occur in the process of transformation will not necessarily be easy. Sometimes those who are most in favor of change go through the most discomfort when change actually takes place. When Charles and I first began working together, he made what turned out to be a prophetic invitation. "Sue," he said, during one of our weekly supervisory sessions, "if there is something you

> **"The best way to deal with 'team ministry hesitation'
> is to get it out in the open and talk about what can be
> done to build better systems and to build mutual
> trust between paid staff and nonpaid staff."**

feel strongly about and you find me or the rest of the staff resisting, I expect you to push back a little." I remember that phrase vividly—"push back a little." I also remember how foreign and even uncomfortable it seemed to me at the time. I, who had grown up in a household of elders (mother and grandparents), instinctively shunned the idea of resisting resistance. In my background, the last thing you were supposed to do with people in leadership was "push back a little."

Fortunately, my work became my passion. And when someone is passionate about a concept or process, he or she often pushes back without even knowing it. There were times in my dealings with Charles when I pushed back more than a little. I am still amazed at how graciously he handled my counterresistance . . . most of the time! He didn't always go along, but he seldom really got in my way. When I pushed back, sometimes he pushed back as well. In fact, he came to give those occasional "push back" moments a descriptive name. They were our "Come to Jesus" sessions.

One of the marks of Charles's leadership throughout these amazing years of transformation has seldom been the wisdom he showed in overruling our errors. Rather, it has been the wisdom he showed in disagreeing when necessary, but also in being willing to let us fail or succeed based on our own passion. We didn't have to have his permission to do well or to do poorly. He was willing to learn from our mistakes as well as from our successes.

CONFLICT MOMENT

WHEN I SPEAK OF the "intense discussions" and even arguments that Charles and I had at times along the way, I often sense an audience getting uncomfortable. I realized early on that conflict in the church is like the proverbial "elephant in the room." The harder we try to avoid talking about it, the more we keep tripping over it!

As a child raised by several adults, including two sets of grandparents, I learned a lot about respect and compliance at a young age. While this was valuable training in the area of family honor, it left me, as a grown woman, with few "conflict resolution" skills. What's more, I learned few of the rough-and-tumble skills that come with experience in the business environment. But as a mother of three, I got hands-on training in the art of mediation. This background had a definite impact on my experience as a director of lay ministries.

As Charles and I moved into various areas of ministry and experienced the inevitable challenges and the occasional differences of perspective, I felt ill equipped to manage certain conflict situations. Additionally, I found many people involved in service who felt guilty whenever there were issues of disagreement, because, after all, this was the church and there shouldn't be any conflict in the church!

Au contraire! Conflict is simply a by-product of people being together. It actually looms larger the more we pretend it doesn't exist.

As part of my continuing education I chose Marlene Wilson's program for certification in nonprofit management at the University of Colorado. At that time it was the only program of its kind. (I'm happy to report that there are many more now.) It was a three-year process that included several week-long intensive courses on a specific topic. For my first intensive, I chose conflict resolution. The class turned out to be the single most significant training I received to equip me for my role as a leader. I returned to my church with a new ability to communicate. I knew how to list and diagnose simple problems in contrast to serious conflicts. I had a much greater awareness of how to catch a problem before it became a full-blown conflict. Naturally, I also became aware that most churches live with a herd of elephants in the living room!

As I always do after returning from a continuing-education opportunity, I reported to Charles on my experience. He shared how he wished he had had such a class to prepare him for his role in leadership. As a follow-up I did some research and found that the Alban Institute sponsored a class on conflict resolution. Charles heartily agreed that we would attend the two-day seminar together. It was a wonderful experience in which we both gained insights into our strengths and weaknesses based on our personal styles and how our styles influenced the way we dealt with conflict. We were so excited about our personal discoveries we felt it would provide a great learning experience for all of our leaders. On the spot we invited the presenter to facilitate a retreat for our ministry leaders and staff members.

As a result of that experience, we learned how to make a separation between issues and people, how to speak a common language to defuse problems before they become conflicts, how to listen for the underlying issues, and how to "speak the truth in love." While the Scriptures apply this standard to all Christians, I find it's not easy to do without proper training. We have to be equipped to speak the truth in love.

Charles and I continued to have our "Come to Jesus" sessions, but we also learned to get better at them. Because we believed in the process and worked hard to understand each other more deeply, the anger often gave way to humor. Along the way, we came up with some paraphrases of Scripture that uniquely applied to our sessions. We learned that "you will know the truth, and the truth will set you free" (John 8:32) sounds good, but it isn't easy. So we got in the habit of reminding ourselves that the truth might first make you really mad—then it will set you free!

EXPERIMENT IN TRAINING

THE NECESSITY FOR TRAINING was a constant topic among those I invited to help with the transformation process. We couldn't think of an area where the training offered to people serving in ministry was sufficient. But this realization came late in the process. We had a lot of systems in place before we realized we were doing a poor job of equipping people for ministry. We were affirming that they could and should do ministry, but when we gave them opportunities, we were failing when it came to setting them up to succeed. We began to think about ways to improve existing training opportunities in order to work out the kinks in the system before we shifted to a training expectation for everyone in ministry.

I recognized that the elders needed training that would be specific to their role (in addition to what Charles had already done to prepare them biblically). When I first broached the subject of a different approach to training, Charles didn't readily agree with my plan. It wasn't that he thought the present training was adequate. The problem was, as he put it, "We're already asking so much of our leaders. I don't think we can ask them for more time."

My argument in response was that we could equip them to be better leaders if we invested the time to provide them with the skill sets and management support that would in the long run save time and help them be more effective in their leadership role.

We were struggling to implement the understanding that one of the core values of the equipping model was the stewardship of time. On that particular occasion, Charles and I were in the same book but not on the same page. We both wanted to guard the time commitments of our church leaders, but each of us had a different idea of how to accomplish it.

I scheduled a training for the elders. When I emphasized to Charles that I needed his support for complete participation by the board, he balked. In fact, he had already received a call from a longtime elder who had asked to be excused from the training session. Charles had agreed that the meeting was unnecessary for experienced leaders. And while he was at it, he excused himself from the meeting, too.

Needless to say, I was upset. It turned into one of those "Come to Jesus" moments. We talked back and forth for a while, but at that point

Charles was not convinced that the elders, particularly those who had served a long time, needed additional training. But, to his credit, he never tried to stop the meeting from going forward.

To my delight and amazement, fifteen of the eighteen members of the elder board showed up for the meeting. I had sent each of them a personal letter of invitation, explaining the specifics of what I expected from the gathering. I told them the meeting would last from 7:00 to 9:00 P.M. and would consist solely of developing skills and tools for their ministry. We would not be dealing with the theology, which they had already heard in an earlier session. My agenda was based on the conversations my team had been having with leaders. Their questions and frustrations provided a helpful guide in planning the content of the meeting.

At that first training session in the new transformational mind-set, we established important ground rules. Right from the outset we did our best to target our training to the specific needs of the group. We answered their questions and provided practical, experience-driven suggestions about their roles. They asked more questions. In fact, once they discovered it was safe to ask, they asked with abandon!

It's important to note that I did not do all the training. Before the initial elder training session took place, I had discovered a gifted trainer in our church body who was the executive vice president of corporate training for a major bank in our community. While I always tried to be careful not to pigeonhole people by profession, I knew that Sally's passion was the training of adults. I invited her to work with me and take a leadership role in the session, with the ongoing purpose of expanding the leadership development area of lay ministries for Brentwood. She embraced the opportunity wholeheartedly.

Sally's teaching gift served our team well. She trained us to be better trainers, and we in turn trained Sally in the biblical foundations and principles that guided our training. It was an enormous "win-win" for both the church and the lay leader. Sally went on to become the first "elder to leadership development" and assisted in developing both a team and effective training opportunities that would serve all areas of the church. And it all went back to her role in the very first elder training session!

We honored our covenant by beginning and ending that first session on time. At 9:00 I informed the group we would conclude the meeting, even though they were still asking questions. I announced that those who wanted to stay were welcome to do so. What a blessing when the group unanimously decided to stay another forty-five minutes because they were enjoying the interaction so much. During the extra time, we were able to ask a few evaluation questions:

- What was helpful about this training session?
- How could we do it better the next time?
- What other needs or areas would you like to have addressed at a future session?

Out of these questions we began to develop our needs-assessment emphasis—which resulted in empowering the present leaders to suggest, out of their struggles and discoveries, ways in which we could train future leaders more effectively. They got the joy of making things easier for the next group!

The morning after the training session Charles received a number of phone calls. Enthusiastic and informed elders with a new sense of confidence about their role in the church were calling him. They expressed a new attitude about the importance of training. Or, to use language in keeping with our biblical model, they had gotten a taste of equipping, and they thought it was great!

Charles taught me a significant lesson in leadership humility when he called me later in the day. I picked up the phone, and he got right to the point in a sheepish tone of voice: "So, I hear you had a pretty good gathering last night." Since I wasn't sure what was coming next, I replied, "Who did you hear that from?" He chuckled and said, "Actually, I've heard it from several places. I've gotten a few phone calls." Then he added words I've heard very few pastors say: "I guess I was wrong about that one, wasn't I?" This admission that he, too, had a lot to learn along the way (a repeated pattern throughout his years of ministry) provided an important behind-the-scenes catalyst in our transformation process. Each of us was getting it wrong sometimes. We were all learning. God was working.

DISAGREEMENT AND TRUST

MY DECISION TO HOLD the training session in spite of my pastor's disagreement created some enduring lessons. I didn't act in such an assertive manner very often, but the fact that I could (and that no matter whether my plan failed or succeeded Charles would acknowledge my effort) affected positively many others in addition to me. We realized we had a pastor who didn't always have to have his way.

Charles's absence from the first training session also affirmed for me the importance of the senior pastor's validation. The value of his or her presence, especially with respect to the strategic leaders of the church, can hardly be measured. This conviction has only grown in me over the years.

This early training success created a significant precedent for my relationship with Charles. I could now point to an example of justified passion and argue in our "Come to Jesus" sessions that I felt strongly about a decision. It was my way of "pushing back a little."

VISION AND TRAINING

A YEAR AFTER THE training session described above, Charles approached me with the new schedule. At the top of his list was the next orientation for the newly elected officers in the church. He invited me to help him with the session. I knew he hadn't forgotten our year-old tango over training, so I said, "Yes, I'd like to be involved. Would you be open to some enhancements for the orientation?"

He responded with equal caution: "What do you have in mind, Mallory?"

I began with something familiar and nonthreatening. "Food would be good," I suggested. "It has a biblical feel to it, you know—Christian leaders sharing around a meal."

He laughed as he responded, "I like that. It just hadn't occurred to me in the context of leadership training."

His openness encouraged me to go on. I had a number of suggestions that came as a result of the year of crash training I had just received, much of it in circles far beyond the local church. I had also heard occasional rumblings within the church that I interpreted as obvious clues that our training needed to improve. But I was keenly aware that I was now treading on hallowed ground. Charles was the senior pastor, and I was giving him input and sharing insights on doing training. (Eventually, although it took years, we came to a mutual conclusion that a void existed in Charles's and many other pastors' seminary background when it came to leadership development and human resource management. I simply had assumed they had skill training in those areas.)

In short, I offered him a plan for the session. The evening would begin at 5:30 P.M. with dinner. At the table we would begin to share our personal stories. This was an effort to build on the principle that teams involved in difficult decision making and visionary leadership gain enormous benefits from deep knowledge of one another. We wanted to demonstrate our conviction that authentic relationships could improve our ability to challenge each other and exercise corporate wisdom on behalf of the church.

We have seen this point proved repeatedly over the years. Without relationships leadership suffers. The church claims to be about relationships. We describe church membership in relational terms. Our relationship with Christ makes us members of his church. Yet how often do we intentionally give attention to the building of relationships within the church?

During that initial dinner training session, we facilitated the sharing of stories. For many of us we were moving into uncharted territory. Charles modeled vulnerability by sharing his story, incorporating the questions we had created. He was genuine and transparent, which set the tone for the rest of us. We asked targeted questions to focus the conversations:

- What was your earliest church experience?
- How did your relationship with Christ begin?
- What have been the high points of your spiritual journey?
- Tell us why you said yes to being called into leadership at this time?

The last phrase of the last question had an amazing and clarifying effect on our discussion. "At this time" got them thinking and talking about all sorts of immediate issues that affected how they would function as leaders. Some were rising to a sudden challenge to grow spiritually. Some were following through on a lengthy process in which God was guiding them into the position they accepted. Some were returning to leadership after a period of grief or rest. Some described their willingness to lead in terms that were very familiar to me—giving back something of what they felt had been given to them.

After dinner we relocated to another area to continue the training. Charles gave an overview of the biblical basis for their leadership roles. He introduced the *Presbyterian Book of Order* and explained that the first year of leadership would include an ongoing exposure to the breadth of its teaching. When Charles finished, he left to go home to his family.

I then directed the group to the notebook I had prepared for each of them. In it they found the church calendar, the current budget, their ministry description, a copy of the long-range strategic plan, and the previous annual report. From 7:00 to 9:00 P.M. I took them through a highly interactive, foundational, and practical orientation for their roles. Charles had already done the training component of the evening; my job was to orient the leaders to the details of their specific roles. So, for example, we reviewed the schedule of meetings for the year. I assisted them by highlighting when certain reports were due, how they should prepare for the budget process, and which leadership training sessions they were expected to attend. They were able to enter into their personal calendars the significant dates for the next twelve months. Together we were organizing ourselves to function effectively.

Leaders don't necessarily need more meetings; they just need the right ones. The elders were already leaders who possessed amazing leadership character and skills. But they did need help in what was for them uncharted territory. By giving them a practical orientation to their new roles, we set them up to succeed. They rewarded us with wise leadership and deeper commitment.

Leaders don't necessarily need more meetings; they just need the right ones.

Charles's presence and participation were crucial. He didn't have to do everything. As the years went by, his pastoral presence became much more exactly that—*pastoral presence*. He had trained others to do the training. He came to pray, to demonstrate interest, and to underscore the value of what we were doing together. Eventually, even his departures from sessions carried a potent message: "I'm here with you because I believe that what we are gathered to do is important for you, but I'm leaving so that you can also understand that I trust the other leaders in this body to carry out their ministry, even in my absence."

TIMING IS EVERYTHING

THE EARLY YEARS AT Brentwood were filled with learning opportunities for me. As my team grew, the learning opportunities expanded. These learning moments resulted more often from our mistakes than from our careful plans.

One of our early overshots was the tendency to train too hard and give people too much too soon. There were a lot of things people didn't need to know until they needed to know it. When we tried to give it to them before they needed it, they often forgot the information and had to be told again anyway. When they came to the point when they needed to know, their attention to the training was always more focused.

We gradually learned about sequential training. We developed our training schedule so that the yearly cycle ran just ahead of the occasions for which the training was needed. In the early years, for example, part of the beginning orientation included a mini-session on "How to Invite Other People into Ministry." This was a significant aspect of our elders' role. Yet here was the reality: The initial orientation took place in October, but the elders did not officially assume their offices until January. By then, the principles about inviting people into ministry were lost in the shuffle of administrative details. In time we came to plan a session on this very topic for the month right after they took office—right about the time they were discovering they couldn't do their ministry alone and would need to find help. The bottom line was this: Once leaders were convinced they could benefit by giving us their time, they were willing to give us more of it.

Practical Challenges
- Interacting for success with support staff
- Operating the office equipment
- Scheduling space in the buildings for meetings
- Inviting others into ministry
- Being a healthy spiritual leader

Common Problems
- Working with difficult people
- Resolving conflicts
- Dealing with burnout
- Balancing family, ministry, and career demands

Equipping Needs
- Strategic planning
- Sharing ministry effectively (a.k.a. delegating)
- Clarifying goals and objectives within a biblical framework
- Evaluating ministry and people
- Training your successor

The pastoral staff members participated in these sessions in the specific areas that highlighted their own gifts for ministry. They led workshops on such topics as prayer and servant leadership. Lay leaders who were commissioned to lead in worship or to serve at the Lord's Supper received detailed practical guidance in the functions of their ministry as worship assistants. These instructions often came out of a context of very real experiences of terror. People who participated in the Lord's Supper for decades have found themselves tongue-tied the first time they were asked to provide leadership in such a holy moment. It's not so much a sense of unworthiness as it is sheer ignorance of the logistics. Once the basics are explained, these leaders often demonstrate a godly authority and sensitivity as they lead others into worship.

LONG-TERM TRAINING

BECAUSE OUR LEADERSHIP ROLES tend to fall into three-year cycles of service, we have tried to gear our training to these cycles. The core components of the training remain the same, with only occasional minor updates. But we continue to offer needs-based, onetime training for issues that are raised or challenges that come up. Sometimes these training experiences are incorporated into the overall training or orientation program for leaders in our church. The session on conflict resolution, for example, began as targeted training for leaders in areas where there had been a history of difficulties, but it became one of the most sought-after workshops in our general training program. We discovered we were addressing one of those issues that was causing havoc, even though many were denying it was a problem. Even the decision to discuss the topic of conflict in a workshop made the whole possibility of confrontation and giving constructive feedback in the church setting more acceptable and beneficial.

We've discovered that those who benefit much from training often make the best future trainers. We cycle our trainers in and out as gifts in specific areas are discovered within the church. The principle that discipleship is a *lifelong* process of applying biblical truth has made a lasting impression on our congregation. People all across the age spectrum find they have ongoing opportunities to be equipped as more effective and faithful disciples of Jesus Christ. God has a place of dignity and service for his children throughout all the days of their lives.

EQUIPPING PRINCIPLES

Declare the Value of Training

Another way to express this principle is this: Lift up the necessity of equipping. The healthy focus on gifts and skills that is gaining ground throughout the church at large will have only limited effectiveness if the idea persists that the only thing people need to know is their gifts and the rest comes automatically. It isn't, and it doesn't. Ephesians 4 makes it clear that some gifts are given for the purpose of equipping. Gifts and equipping are not the same thing. Very gifted people still need training.

So how do we declare the value of training? We do so by making training a requirement for, a prerequisite of, the invitation into ministry, especially for leadership roles. After we discover people's gifts and identify a match between the gifts and an opportunity for ministry, we invite people to prayerfully consider the opening. Part of the invitation (and what often makes it appealing to those who are moving into ministry for the first time) is the commitment on the part of the church to train those we invite into ministry. We promise that if God has led them to assume these responsibilities, then our responsibility will be to equip them with skills, materials, resources, and support in their effort. If they say yes, are we ready to train them?

Acknowledge Different Learning Styles

Training is not just another meeting! What we discovered about our elders has held true all across the church: People don't need more meetings; they simply need the right ones. We are charged to be good stewards of our people's time.

Effective training acknowledges that not everyone learns the same way. Some learn by trial and error, others want detailed instructions. Some can listen and apply; others need to interact. Some need to see it, others need to feel it, and still others need to hear it. The temptation is to train in one way and in only one way, and it tends to tilt toward the learning style most comfortable for the person doing the training. But that one way will be effective with only a small percentage of our people. What often happens is that everyone else quickly develops low expectations about training.

At the very least, incorporate three or four distinctly different approaches to the same content during your training. If the concept of different learning styles is new to you, get training yourself. Think and pray about the particular learning styles of the specific group you are training before you plan the session. To get leaders to become stakeholders in ministry and to understand the DNA of your church, you must invest in them, equip them, and raise the bar of accountability. The results will be amazing!

Target Training to Respond to Culture, Values, and Needs

Similar to the principle of acknowledging different learning styles is the companion principle of targeted training. The kind of training cycle and the specific training events we developed at Brentwood take into account a dual emphasis on (1) broad training in the purposes of the church, the details of general discipleship, and the importance of corporate worship and (2) specific skill sets and orientation that particular roles require. Our daylong training sessions seek to keep a balance between the two components above. Create training to respond to your culture, your values, and the needs of your people as they live out their calling to serve.

Discover the Felt Needs and Objective Needs

Felt needs are the expectations and questions that people bring into any situation. *Objective needs* are the actual content and fundamental necessities that people must receive in a given situation.

When this equation impacts training, it creates the following tension: The trainer knows what specific knowledge and skills the trainee requires for the job; the trainee brings certain fears, doubts, questions, experiences, and insights that will greatly influence his or her capacity to respond to the training.

When leaders are reluctant to participate in training, you can be certain that they don't expect either their felt needs or the objective needs to be met. Here's the key to overcoming reluctance: Discover what they think and feel they need, and offer it to them. Watch for ways you can invite them to help shape the sessions and the content. The best training will be a blend of what they want to know and what you want them to know. For more about this, see the equipping principle "Record Needs Assessment" below.

Be sure, then, also to train and equip leaders to know how to deal effectively with conflict resolution. People often need help grasping the principle that unless you get to a win-win solution, you have not resolved the conflict. For where two or three are gathered . . . there will eventually be a conflict that needs resolution! Let us not ignore the elephants. Let us also not assume that conflict resolution is a natural skill practiced by our leaders. Assumptions like this continue to be the kiss of death for truth, honesty, and an effective witness in the church.

Begin and End Meetings on Time

Church meetings are notorious for their length. The law of diminishing returns often operates in church meetings: The length of time spent in the meeting is in opposite proportion to the amount of significant work accomplished. Show your people that you really value their time by starting and stopping on time.

Open-ended church meetings usually generate low response. People no longer live in a world of open-ended commitments. Discretionary time is the valued currency of our day. As leaders, we must be good stewards of that time. People will make more informed decisions about their participation if they know up front what will be discussed and how much time has been allotted for the discussion.

Record Needs Assessment

For each role in your church structure, ask yourself: Is there a record somewhere of what a person actually needs to know in order to perform this function effectively? If not, how do you get to that place? Here are a couple of tools we've found helpful in building role expectations and descriptions and in developing training models:

- An *exit interview* provides a wealth of information based on personal experience. Future leaders can benefit immensely, even from the frustrations and failures of past leaders. Exit interviews take the fresh observations of a departing leader and use them to prepare his or her replacement.
- A *needs assessment* is all about asking the right questions. The skills required of the interviewer are effective listening and the ability to feed back for clarification the intent of the statement. All good assessments, whether written or oral, should include a "general comments" and "felt needs" section. Other people can easily assume that leaders (even those who have been leaders for a long time) possess a certain knowledge or training experience, and consequently they may overlook genuine felt needs that have never been addressed. If you take the time to ask and listen, you will often be surprised by the genuine needs of those you are inviting into ministry.

Set Them Up to Succeed

The underlying and critical foundation for everything we do in the area of equipping people must be the goal to set them up to succeed. Invite them in a way that gives them a sense that they can *succeed* in doing what you are inviting them to do. Structure their role description to ensure success. Craft your training with several questions in mind:

- What do they need to know in order to succeed?
- What do they need from the church in order to succeed?
- How can we help define success in such a way that they will experience some?
- How will we recognize and celebrate their large and small successes?

EQUIPPING HEROES

Heartland Community Church
Overland Park, Kansas
www.heartlandchurch.org
Senior Pastor: Craig McElvain
Equipping Pastor: Glenn Kahler

One of the most exciting and reportable models I have seen for intentional leadership development is at Heartland Community Church. Using the language of sports from beginning to end, their program is called the "Farm Team." The value of leadership development came from the senior pastor and is validated by the presence of a staff person whose job is to train leaders.

Equipping pastor Glenn Kahler described the initial driving motivation as a "painful need" recognized by the staff. They saw the need to take responsibility for identifying and developing future leaders in order to fill a void. Recognizing that the value had to be modeled from the top down to be authentic, they initially targeted the elders and key existing leaders.

As the church grew, the core leadership team needed to reproduce more and more leaders for every area of ministry. Both the equipping pastor and the senior pastor, Craig McElvain, came up through the Young Life ministry and built on their experiences. One of their core realities stated that in order to be in ministry, you had to enlist and equip volunteers. They designed a summer internship program with college kids that eventually served as the model for the church's leadership development program (the Farm Team). It is clearly a discipleship model with a wonderfully expanded focus on being relevant and responsive to the world they serve.

Glenn Kahler states that "whoever provides an arena for leadership development will find leaders." It's a bit of the mentality of "build it, and they will come." Heartland created a leadership culture by raising the bar of expectations, accountability, and church investment in growing her people. One joins the Farm Team by personal invitation from a staff member. When I asked Glenn how these Farm Team members were identified, he said the staff processes the question, "Which of your developing volunteers show potential to be key leaders?" The leadership development commitment begins in October and concludes in May and involves weekly meetings in a small-group setting where team members work, share their stories, pray, and grow together. They study the Scriptures, as well as the values and the culture of their community of faith (their DNA), and they are expected to read ten additional books on a broad range of topics.

The four primary principles of Farm Team training are as follows:

1. Model spiritual maturity
2. Carry the vision banner
3. Mentor others
4. Truly fulfill your ministry call

Each individual engaged in leadership development is on a pathway to becoming a key leader and needs to understand and accept the fact that he or she will have a large responsibility. The training culminates with a retreat that includes a graduation ceremony at which they receive their future ministry assignment.

Follow-up is critical and intentional, incorporating such questions as, "Are you in the right place? Is this a good fit? Is it necessary to relocate?" Only about 10 percent of the initial connections require a redirection. One of the additional values of the Farm Team commitment is that the new and emerging leaders learn and claim the DNA of the church and have a better understanding and ownership of the vision, culture, and direction of the church in which they will be leading.

The culture of Heartland is based on a commitment to coaching and growing people; staff members accept the commitment as part of their role, and it is named in their job descriptions and addressed in their performance evaluations. The senior pastor makes this his top priority, rearranges his schedule as needed to mentor apprentice leaders, and oftentimes has to take things off his plate in order to practice these values.

QUESTIONS FOR REFLECTION AND DISCUSSION

1. How are you setting up your leaders to succeed?

2. Reflect on your attitude toward people in the pews. Do you see them as diamonds in the rough, waiting to be polished, or do you see them as lumps of coal?

3. What role is the church playing in polishing these diamonds?

4. What is your plan for ongoing leadership development? How does it address the felt needs of those who are called to serve?

10

Viewing the Vision of Three Equipping Churches

He handed out gifts of apostle, prophet, evangelist, and pastor-teacher to train Christians in skilled servant work, working within Christ's body, the church, until we're all moving rhythmically and easily with each other, efficient and graceful in response to God's Son, fully mature adults, fully developed within and without, fully alive like Christ.

Ephesians 4:11-13 THE MESSAGE

BY NOW IT MAY seem obvious, but the Ephesians passage places a much greater emphasis on roles than on shape. When we think of the church body in a particular place, the specific shape she takes in that community must be a combination of the culture of that community and the values of Scripture. Christ gets to determine the specific shape, since the body belongs to him!

The mode of church planting that transplants the church whole from one culture to another never quite works. The church remains foreign, or she changes to fit the culture. What preserves her as Christ's body is the degree to which Christ's purposes and character are seen in the unique relationships that develop among people.

The questions we need to ask in exploring our faithfulness to the biblical model are these:

- To what degree are we producing people who are "fully alive like Christ"?
- What needs to change in order to reach this goal?

Churches that diligently seek to live out their answers to these questions take on unique forms. Given the opportunity, Christ really does shape his body.

"METHODS ARE MANY, principles are few; methods always change, principles never do." Wayne Cordeiro, pastor of New Hope Christian Fellowship in Oahu, Hawaii, speaks the truth in this nugget of equipping wisdom. Not only does the local vision of an equipping church undergo continuous revision in practice, but every local example of the equipping church will be unique as well. The principles will be the same; the particular methods, shape, and color of the principles with respect to the way they are applied will vary.

"Methods are many, principles are few; methods always change, principles never do."

Let me illustrate by describing three different churches, all of them deeply committed to the biblical principles of living as equipping churches. Although they happen to share common denominational affiliation (United Methodist), they are radically different churches located in Ohio, Kansas, and Texas. Two of these churches experienced transformation as well-established congregations; one was newly planted in 1990. Two of them chose to identify themselves by their location—Ginghamsburg Church and Windsor Village Church. The third was planted by a small group of people who began meeting in a funeral parlor and thought it only fitting that they call themselves the Church of the Resurrection.

Ginghamsburg Church

Ginghamsburg Church's current pastor, Michael Slaughter, arrived in Tipp City, Ohio, in 1979, when the church was already over a hundred years old. Less than ninety members were keeping a wonderful tradition alive. In the first century of ministry this particular church had sent out more than fifty young people into pastoral ministry.

Mike clearly remembers an experience on an April day in 1979 when he walked out in the field behind the little two-room country church and said to God, "I'm not going to leave this field until I have a vision of what you want this church to be." During the course of that day in the field, God gradually began giving Mike the components of a vision—a hope for the future. Among those components were the following:

- a picture of three thousand people worshiping together
- a church known as a teaching center that was helping to influence and challenge other churches
- a genuine, multiracial body of Christ
- a church that empowered God's people
- a church in which people were introduced to a personal relationship with Jesus Christ and invited to serve him in the structures of society

Mike's passion for his vision set in motion a number of changes that began to be implemented over time. Worship music became more contemporary. The work that went into maintaining the organization was streamlined, and efforts to impact the community for Christ were emphasized. For example, they instituted a one-night-per-month rule in which the church's administrative meetings all took place during one evening of the month. This was intentionally done to free up people to pursue personal ministry in their families and in the community. Not surprisingly, some changes occurred at the church as a result of the new direction. A number of people left the church—about a third of the membership. The church got leaner on her way to living out her vision effectively.

As the first year unfolded, Mike followed a three-part strategy:

1. He taught from the Scriptures about the character of the community and about God's expectations for the church.
2. He oversaw the downsizing (or, as Mike terms it, "rightsizing") of the church.
3. He began to disciple a leadership team.

Mike focused his preaching on Acts 2:38, emphasizing repentance, a new way of living based on the "dying" principle enacted in baptism (see also Romans 6:3–4), and the principle of the church participating in supernatural ministry. Church members came to an agreement to stop looking at opportunities from the narrow perspective of a little church and begin seeing opportunities from the large perspective of Almighty God. They decided to conduct life on the truth that God blesses what the church does by faith, not by sight.

One of the church's first practical long-range decisions was that if any subject under discussion was something Jesus would do, then his disciples could not vote no. Mike says, "That's how to grow a budget from $27,000 a year to $5 million a year. God's not impressed by or pressed to provide either amount. God blesses those who risk in faith."

When Mike began to disciple the initial leadership team, the invitation to participate had only two conditions: regular attendance and the willingness to reproduce in the lives of other people what they were learning. That original small group (or "circle of caring") turned out to be the key to what has happened at Ginghamsburg. When Mike describes the history of their transformation, he begins with that small group. He calls it their introduction to the practice of *koinonia*—genuine Christian fellowship.

Ginghamsburg promotes the idea of team in their concept of ministry all across the body of Christ. Mike describes the structure this way:

> Team culture is not a hierarchy with one leader leading other leaders who lead other leaders. The structure is horizontal. People come together and function based on their gifts and anointing by God. In team, one plus one doesn't equal two. The effect of two working in tandem is exponential. They can accomplish much more together than they could ever accomplish apart.

Even such traditionally "solo" aspects of church life such as preaching are carried out by a team at Ginghamsburg. This doesn't mean that people take turns preaching; it means that a group of people gifted in various media, as well as other specially gifted ministry people, are in on every aspect of developing every worship service. Visuals used during the sermon recognize that not everyone learns the same way. A team works all week to plan every worship service. Mike reports that something amazing happens when a team plans as compared to one person.

When asked about the church's core, Mike lifts up the biblical doctrine of the priesthood of all believers. Ginghamsburg Church emphasizes the ministry of all members. He estimates that among the more than seventy people who are on staff at the church, all but five came up "through the ranks." The church has become a training ground for wider, deeper ministry. Mike elaborates:

> That's how we've developed our staff—based on their giftedness. We have helped them to develop into the full purpose God has for their life and the calling for which they were created. In short, that is my mission statement: to connect people to their God-destiny. That's why we exist. To help people discover their own burning bush. And then we throw gasoline on that burning bush.

When asked what advice he would give to other pastors about leading a local church toward becoming an equipping body, Mike highlights three points:

1. Take time to really listen to God, and ask what God's vision is for the church.
2. Cultivate a deep relationship with Jesus Christ.
3. Become a student of culture; get to know the people Christ has sent you to reach.

> "That is my mission statement: to connect people
> to their God-destiny. That's why we exist.
> To help people discover their own burning bush.
> And then we throw gasoline on that burning bush."

Ginghamsburg has responded to opportunities to be a teaching church, opening her doors to people from other places who are seeking to see an equipping church in action. The more than three thousand members of the church are having a worldwide impact for Christ. To find out more about this church, visit their Web site at www.ginghamsburg.org.

Church of the Resurrection

The Church of the Resurrection was planted in 1990 in Leawood, Kansas, by a young seminarian named Adam Hamilton. From a humble beginning where worship took place in a funeral parlor, this church has grown to more than six thousand members. Similar to Ginghamsburg Church, this church sees herself as a reproducible, teaching church. Part of her vision is to provide a model for revitalized spiritual growth within a mainline denomination that has experienced extensive loss of membership.

When I visited Church of the Resurrection's facilities and spoke with Adam and his staff, I came away with a number of impressions. The pastor is a hometown boy who has made excellent use of his formative memories. He knows the culture of the people he is leading. During the early days of the church start-up, he developed the life of the church by asking himself this question, "What didn't I like about church as I was growing up?"

Wherever those dislikes related to a structure or method, he explored with his people some other way of accomplishing the same purpose. The excuses most people use to turn away from church he employed to reshape the church. In planning these changes, he has kept in mind the importance of highlighting the core doctrines and biblical teaching that brought him to Christ.

I was impressed with the clear vision that the church presents to newcomers. Church of the Resurrection presents herself with strong visual images that capture the imagination and inspire curiosity. Church members use the language of mountain climbing to help explain the Christian life. Their definition of discipleship incorporates the idea of an individual attaining a summit and then returning to the valley to guide others to the top. The church's entire program is explained by use of climbing terms, including the point of entry or connection for any person. Visitors are invited to consider where they are in relation to the Christian life:

spectators, novices, explorers, enthusiasts, or guides. The Sunday school classes and other Christian education opportunities are open to anyone, but they are organized and promoted as particularly suitable to certain levels of climbers. The emphasis on growth, change, and discipleship is apparent within moments after entering the facilities.

The church's strong vision carries over into her identity as a teaching church. Not only is she intent on providing ongoing spiritual summits for her members through the UpWord Bound University (UBU), but the church has also intentionally invited other congregations to send representatives to her School of Congregational Development, where church members share what they are learning with other churches going through the process of transformation. In so doing Church of the Resurrection is having a powerful influence in many present and future congregations scattered across the nation.

What I found most encouraging about Church of the Resurrection (COR) is her clear presentation of discipleship expectations for each member. Some of the core objectives are as follows:

- to raise up and equip servant leaders within the church
- to develop new models for ministry
- to reinforce collaboration among clergy, staff, and laity to accomplish God's purposes
- to provide pathways for Christian service outside of Church of the Resurrection

Continual opportunities for growth are kept before the congregation. These are reinforced by expecting growing disciples to meet prerequisites before further training. The pathway to the summit of spiritual maturity has clear markers. For example, enrollment in UBU, which has a registration fee, also has the following requirements: a Bible survey course, regular weekly worship attendance, an active role in some ministry for at least a year, the completion of spiritual gifts discovery, and a desire to become a deeply committed disciple of and leader for Christ. The atmosphere of serious spiritual growth is refreshing indeed!

The atmosphere of welcoming change and adaptation that made planting a church so exciting continues to be alive and well at Church of the Resurrection. Adam remains committed to pursuing the development of strong teams of leaders who will keep the church on the right path. You can discover more about this dynamic church by visiting her Web site at www.cor.org.

Windsor Village Church

Pastor Kirbyjon Caldwell has served Windsor Village United Methodist Church for more than seventeen years. The church, on the southwest side of Houston, Texas, has grown from 25 to 12,000 members. Unlike the other two churches I've just described, Windsor Village serves an urban population. Among the features that make Windsor Village unique is the wide variety of practical ministries that have sprung up within the church but serve the community at large. Over one hundred different ministries, many of them functioning as 503(c)(3) nonprofit organizations, make a tremendous impact throughout the community.

When asked to distinguish an equipping, lay-driven church from a staff-driven church, Kirbyjon responds with discernment:

> That's a good question. I think Windsor Village has been both a CEO-influenced and a lay-driven church. Let me tell you what I mean by that. It's been CEO influenced from the standpoint that I have always viewed myself as the one who's primarily responsible for casting the vision. And I think that over the course of time, as successful visions have been cast, the laypersons have looked to me, either intentionally or unintentionally, to stay one vision ahead of them. From the point of "change agenting," I'm the one with the primary responsibility.

Yet Kirbyjon proceeds quickly to talk about the positive features of being a lay-driven church:

> Well, none of the change associated with the vision would have taken place had it not been for competent, caring, consistent, and compassionate laypersons. The people here at Windsor are not only responsible for implementing a vision, they're also responsible for creating mini-visions, if you will, for their respective ministries and departments. Of course, every mini-vision has to be compatible with the major vision.

When asked about the challenges facing the senior pastor of an equipping church, Kirbyjon summarizes two key points: identify the right people to place in leadership, and trust them. "If you're going to meet the needs of folk and fulfill the kingdom in the twenty-first century," notes Kirbyjon, "then you must learn how to enroll and involve the appropriate personnel. And that involves trust."

Windsor Village Church has boldly moved toward the needs of people in an urban environment. The members have shaped their responses to those needs by obeying Jesus and taking action. They sponsor a large community center called the Power Center. This community resource, which employs about two hundred people, provides medical, educational, financial, and entrepreneurial services to the community. The Power Center began with a thousand-dollar loan and a compelling vision to meet needs. It is involved in developing a planned community that will eventually provide over 450 homes in an environment that will promote the gospel message.

"The key to keeping the equipping vision alive," says Kirbyjon, "is to be committed to change." He acknowledges that while not many will confess to enjoying change, it is inevitable, especially in these times. He adds, "We will not be able to be who God is calling us to be without change. I'd even suggest that without change the church will die. So either you choose to change, or you choose to die." For more information on this lively and bold church, visit www.kingdombuilder.com.

"The key to keeping the equipping vision alive is to be committed to change."

POINTS IN COMMON

THOUGH THESE THREE CHURCHES are very different in their particular identity, they all share a common heritage of being United Methodist. They celebrate the warm evangelical dynamics that were the hallmark of the Wesleyan movement in the past centuries. They see themselves as inheritors of the bold equipping ministry that swept across the nation in the past and established so many churches in pioneer environments that even today there are still more Methodist churches in the United States than post offices.

These three churches illustrate that churches with a common heritage can and do turn out unique models as they apply the truthful principles that govern the body of Christ.

FIND YOUR OWN MODEL

DURING THE YEARS I've been presenting this equipping model, I've had the privilege of finding the model to be alive and well in many very different churches. I say with great confidence that you should be able to identify several congregations in your denomination that are already involved in applying these principles. Look at the congregations that are growing; contact people there and ask them what is going on. If they can talk intelligently about their church, you may have uncovered an equipping church. Keep talking with them. Listen for evidence that the people own the ministry of their church. Someone may talk with great excitement about a charismatic leader or about a particular ministry within a church that for the most part is dead, but when you find a large percentage of people living into their gifts and calling, and when they show that they're a part of the team that leads the church, then you have identified an equipping church. Where people in the pews are excited about their role in the body of Christ, you can be sure that in some way the priesthood of believers is being experienced and Christians are being equipped for ministry.

EQUIPPING PRINCIPLES

Process-ors Last for the Marathon

People who apply these principles will usually fall into two groups: the program-ers and the process-ors. Those who see the equipping model as a surefire program that their church can "plug and play" will inevitably become discouraged and frustrated. Oh, you can make it into a program all right—and even do it in a relatively short period of time—but it won't be long before you'll be looking for another quick fix, and the church will have added a suitcase of equipping stuff to go with the rest of the baggage.

The process-ors have learned that real change doesn't happen overnight. Most of the principles I've outlined in this book take months and even years of patient commitment to implement. If you're not convinced that a passion for equipping ministry is your biblical mandate, you may not endure the marathon.

The churches I've described in this chapter are where they are today as a result of years of work by committed teams of people who were originally inspired with a great vision that has stood the test of time.

Wait for the Compounding Effect

You don't need to work as an investment banker or possess a degree in economics to appreciate a basic principle of long-term savings: When you are earning interest for your monetary investment, the growth at first is painfully slow; but after a certain point, the compounding effect becomes obvious, and the rate of accumulation increases dramatically.

The equipping principles in Scripture function the same way. If the vision becomes the passion of a small team of people in the church who are willing to practice the principles over the long haul, the compounding effect will eventually be seen. The churches profiled in this chapter had numerical growth as part of their vision, but because they placed the spiritual growth and maturity of members as a top value, the numerical growth that eventually occurred was evidence of the spiritual compounding effect.

Begin Your Own Local Network

I don't think I can overemphasize the importance of seeking out others who are committed to the equipping process. Consider attending a Leadership Training Network seminar; it will be, among other things, a golden opportunity to connect with others from your denomination or geographic area who are seeking to apply these biblical principles in their churches.

Let me tell you something about people who are committed to the equipping process: They don't keep their experiences a secret. The principles to which they are committed obligate them to share. Real equippers want to encourage other equippers! Begin your own local network of equipping leaders for the purpose of supporting, learning from, and collaborating with one another.

EQUIPPING HEROES

The senior pastors and the staff members at Ginghamsburg Church, Church of the Resurrection, and Windsor Village Church are all equipping heroes. They are literally talking the talk and walking the walk of equipping ministry. They are working through the day-by-day trials and tribulations that come even when they know they're doing what is right and good. They are fighting the good fight, keeping the faith, and equipping others to carry on!

QUESTIONS FOR REFLECTION AND DISCUSSION

1. Aside from the obvious fact that they are part of the same denomination, what characteristics do these equipping churches have in common?

2. Look for churches in your community that are vital and healthy. Call, connect, have an intentional conversation, and listen well to discover the elements of health. As you do, evaluate the vitality and health of your own church.

3. Are you caught in the "yeah, but" mentality—saying "*yeah, but* these are all big churches and I just have a small church"? If so, go back and reread this chapter. How many people did Mike Slaughter begin with? Adam Hamilton? Kirbyjon Caldwell? Reflect on the uniquely different characteristics that allow for growth.

11

Perpetuating the Transformed Vision

He handed out gifts of apostle, prophet, evangelist, and pastor-teacher to train Christians in skilled servant work, working within Christ's body, the church, until we're all moving rhythmically and easily with each other, efficient and graceful in response to God's Son, fully mature adults, fully developed within and without, fully alive like Christ.

Ephesians 4:11–13 THE MESSAGE

EACH TIME WE'VE COME to Ephesians 4 we've focused on individual words and sections of Paul's picture of the equipping church. Can we take it all in at once? Are the terms and phrases in this passage so rich that we can't see the whole for the parts? How can we step back and see the panoramic view of this marvelous work in progress that God has designed to accomplish his purposes in the world. We admit our incapacity. We agree with Paul that at best we see a poor reflection as in a mirror (see 1 Corinthians 13:12). We see a part of what only God can truly and fully see.

How, then, do we cast a vision? How do we help people see more of the body of Christ in action when they've only had a chance to catch a glimpse? I'm convinced we see it best, most clearly, as we follow the stories of people and the way God works in and through the church to change their lives.

COULD IT HAPPEN AT MY CHURCH?

ALTHOUGH MANY OF THE concepts I've introduced in this book are not new, people need to see that they work! When I stand before people from **179** very different Christian traditions and begin to speak about our experiences at Brentwood, I get a lot of feedback as I look into many pairs of eyes in which I see such intense longing! Many pastors and laypeople approach me at the breaks or after a session and say, with a broad smile on their faces, "Those sure are wonderful stories. Brentwood sounds like a great church. . . ." Their compliment trails off in a wistful sort of way.

They would never guess how glad I am that they came over. But I don't want to overwhelm them. "Yes, they are, and yes, it is!" I respond.

A short, awkward silence follows while they search for a way to say what they need to say without offending me.

"I've got to tell you, though, I doubt those things could ever happen at *my* church."

Now I can't help but smile. They have no idea how far God has brought them already in the short trip from their chair to this conversation. I say, "I hear that a lot. These stories kind of make you feel a little helpless? Like maybe this is too big a task for you to even think about doing?"

"Yeah, I guess that's part of it."

"Well, tell me more. What else is part of it?"

At this point the conversation takes one of several well-worn tracks. For many, personal inadequacy is a huge barrier. They can't imagine God using them anywhere in such a transformational vision. For others, their church seems so entrenched, so hardened to change, that they are tempted to hopelessness. Some have been burned so many times by add-on programs that promised notable change only to become another piece of baggage on an overloaded vehicle. Some are disappointed that I'm not offering a plug-and-play structure to create the instant equipping church. But almost all of them share this deep desire: They want to be part of a church that is showing the world a true answer to questions of meaning and a true pathway to fruitful living.

What a delight now, years later, to count these leadership-training-break conversations as the beginning point of a number of friendships. How exciting to hear, at the close of a training session, the first whispers of a vision for their church! How heartwarming to see them back at another training event with several wide-eyed companions who are beginning to understand the passion of their leader. How energizing to see God doing an amazing work of introducing the original plan once again in church after church across this country.

Each of these persons is living a story of transformation. Each represents a church that is living with transformation. But it all goes back to individual people through whom God works. Someone (maybe you?) has to be passionate about the vision for the church to be all she can be. The vision, like the church herself, must be larger than the individual. I've had the privilege of watching senior pastors, associates, directors of lay ministries, and even people who have no title at all leave our training sessions with a vision much larger than their own abilities and resources. They left with a deeper commitment to trust God, God's Word, and his plans for the church even in the midst of their own personal limitations.

In and through our helpless availability God does his best work. As the apostle Paul put it so eloquently after his own struggle with inadequacy, "But [the Lord] said to me, 'My grace is sufficient for you, for my power is made perfect in weakness'" (2 Corinthians 12:9).

PART OF THE REST OF THE STORY

AT THE BEGINNING OF this book I shared a significant transition in my own life, as I experienced the effects of the body of Christ reaching out in very practical and tangible ways. When I think about the ways in which God's grace can be experienced, I always remember the days of helplessness I lived through in the early 1980s. Little did I know then that God was setting me up.

If back then God had given me any idea of where I would find myself today and what I would be doing, I probably would have had a heart attack. God knew it was enough of a challenge just to think about tomorrow's tasks. Besides, there were many lessons to learn along the way before I was even in a place where I could appreciate some of the irony and humor of God's plan in my life! Along the way, God has provided amazing traveling companions.

The next major transition in my life began in 1993 when I received a letter from Leadership Network, an organization unknown to me at the time. They formally invited me to participate in what they called a forum on spiritual gifts at Glen Eryie, the Navigators facility in Colorado Springs, Colorado. I had some time set aside for study leave, and I was anxious to learn more about spiritual gifts, so I accepted the invitation.

When I arrived, I discovered I was one of about seventy-five people in attendance. The largest subgroup was made up of senior pastors from large churches. Another group consisted of "tool providers"—people who developed techniques and tools for gifts assessments and other kinds of inventories. Many were names I recognized but had never met. I soon realized I was in good company. My mentor, Marlene Wilson, a pioneer in lay mobilization from the volunteer management perspective, was present, as well as three fellow practitioners who were serving in capacities similar to my own in their churches. There was also a handful of people I later came to see as "high-capacity," gifted laypeople.

The forum approach was new to me, and I wasn't sure what to think when, upon my arrival, I was invited to host one of four small groups in which I would share the details of what we were doing at Brentwood. Each practitioner had been asked to host a small group discussion. It was an unexpected invitation, but talking about what was going on at Brentwood was a delightful opportunity for me. The groups rotated members one time, so I shared our story and answered questions with two different small groups. The morning flew by. The good news was that I didn't know any of the people, nor did I realize the depth and breadth of national leadership present, so I was not at all nervous! During the afternoon, the tool providers had their wares on display and answered questions in the same rotating small group format.

Late in the afternoon I discovered why the high-capacity laypeople had been invited to attend. These were highly gifted and capable people who, to one degree or another, felt they were not being used effectively in their churches. They were formed into a panel and were given the following instructions by the moderator: "Here's your chance. We've gathered a number of the most dynamic senior pastors in the country, and we understand you have some comments and concerns you'd like to communicate to them as willing laypeople who want to serve Christ in your churches. What do you want to say?"

One after another the panel members shared pain, frustration, and anger over what they perceived as a rebuff by their church leaders. It wasn't that they were unwilling to do menial tasks such as folding bulletins or passing the offering plates. But they were willing and able to do so much more, and they weren't being permitted or invited to by their pastors. They were not being invited into leadership responsibilities.

Alongside the occasionally defensive responses by the senior pastors present, the tool providers kept insisting that the apparent conflict could be resolved if only their assessment tools would be used so that these people could identify their gifts and thereby find a place where they could fit. At this point I found myself entering the fray. I simply said that our experience at Brentwood certainly affirmed the value of using assessment tools, but they were only a part of a much larger process of care, preparation, leadership development, invitation, and recognition that needed to happen within the church. It wasn't enough to know your gifts. (In the back of my mind I was dreaming about how to get several of these high-capacity people to relocate to our area—we would certainly have a warm welcome waiting at Brentwood!)

This kind of frank confrontation led to quite a bit of tension in the air. The tool providers were still insisting that their forms and questionnaires could solve the problem. I bit my lip to keep from pointing out

What does the church need in order to be healthy, vital, and thriving in the twenty-first century?

that most of the people on the panel were well aware of their gifts. *That* was the point of frustration. They weren't being invited to use them! Such was the mood as the moderator closed the meeting and informed us that we would reconvene the next day.

On Sunday morning the session began with a time of Bible study and prayer. It was a great reminder that God had a purpose in what we were doing together. We were then led in a brainstorming time focused on the question, "What does the church need in order to be healthy, vital, and thriving in the twenty-first century?" As we made suggestions, they were written on sheets of flip-chart paper that were then placed on the wall of the meeting room. The moderator drew out of us an amazing assortment of suggestions.

Each of us was then given the task to name what we considered the top four challenges facing the church in the new century. One of these was, of course, "equipping and developing laity." The overall top vote-getters would become the focal points for four groups over the course of the next several hours. I had no trouble choosing the group under the equipping banner.

Imagine my surprise, then, when Brad Smith, a director in Leadership Network, came over and asked me to facilitate our discussion. I nearly had a stroke. My mentor, Marlene Wilson, was also part of that group, and I pointed out to Brad that she would be a much better facilitator. He insisted that I serve in this role, so I swallowed my terror and forged ahead.

This was our assignment: Assume that time and money are no obstacle. Create a mission, a vision, a dream, and an action plan that would result in a church meeting the challenge of equipping and developing the laity.

This was our assignment: Create a mission, a vision, a dream, and an action plan that would result in a church meeting the challenge of equipping and developing the laity.

The other three practitioners were in our group, along with Marlene and several senior pastors, laypeople, and tool designers—a wonderful cross section of the larger group—all with a heartfelt desire to empower and equip God's people. We created a dream scenario. I will never forget the atmosphere of energy, shared experience, biblical truth, and excitement that flowed in our group. The model we described became not so much an idea for a single church as a model for the church at large. We acknowledged the importance of local factors, but emphasized the universal principles we were rediscovering in Scripture and confirming in our churches. We envisioned a vast movement of churches that would be known for their passion for equipping ministry. We sketched the outline of an organization designed to train pastors and church leaders in the specific areas of equipping ministry that were being neglected in the formal training of clergy. The point was not to compete with seminary training, but to complement that preparation with biblical application and practical insights gleaned from local church experiences.

We even suggested that regional conferences and a national identity would be helpful components in making our dream come to reality. I still think of those hours with a sense of wonder. Most of the ideas generated that morning have lived on in what was to become Leadership Training Network!

The host of the forum event was a man named Bob Buford. After the four presentations had been made, he invited me to have lunch at his table. He asked me about my experiences at Brentwood, and I quickly discovered in listening to his story that he was one of those very high-capacity (and frustrated) laypeople who retained an enormous hope for the local church. At one point he asked in a very casual way, "Do you really think that's possible?"

"Is what really possible?" I responded.

"The vision your group dreamed up this morning," he said.

In my usual cautious way I said, "Absolutely! In a heartbeat!"

I was about to discover why Bob's special gift as a godly man includes funding ministry dreams and initiatives. He responded to my enthusiasm with an invitation to participate in a group meeting immediately following the forum whose specific purpose would be to pursue our equipping vision in greater detail. Bob hosted Brad, Marlene, a couple of other people, and me as we discussed what it would take to launch an organization designed to promote this vision.

I was certainly honored to participate in the meeting. We discussed a number of action steps, including getting together at future meetings, identifying other key people to invite into involvement, and highlighting organizational principles we wanted to be sure to preserve. I thought Marlene would be a perfect leader for such a movement. However, Marlene was just entering into a yearlong sabbatical, and her gifts and interests still lay in the national arena of volunteer management in which she had a number of goals yet to pursue

As disappointed as I was in not being able to work alongside Marlene in developing this vision, I was also not prepared to accept the leadership opportunity offered to me. Although the possibility of seeing the principles we had practiced at Brentwood transplanted to other congregations was a personal dream, I did not feel qualified for such a directing role. I had minimal academic qualifications. My training had been mostly on-the-job. How could I design and lead an organization that would have national influence? Thus, several times I turned down the offer to take the lead position for the fledgling Leadership Training Network (LTN).

I now see that God used several people and events to guide me in a new direction. An ongoing dialogue with Brad Smith helped me put issues of ministry into perspective, as I benefited from his different theological background, insightful listening, and challenging friendship. Bob Buford patiently listened to all my excuses for saying no to the LTN opportunity (which boiled down to my claim of the lack of academic credentials and qualifications), and his response took me by surprise: "Don't talk to me about credentials or qualifications. You have the gifts and the passion." Bob Shank (at the time senior pastor at South Coast Community Church) preached an extraordinary sermon at a Leadership Network conference on the ministry of Aquila and Priscilla, two New Testament laypeople who teamed with Paul the apostle to form a dynamic ministry team. He then shared how God had led him into ministry in spite of lack of formal training. It seemed to be a sermon designed for me.

In an uncanny way, I sensed all the same components falling into place that were part of what originally led me into ministry at Brentwood. Bob Buford treated my qualifications very much like Charles had done almost a decade earlier. I felt the same sense of helplessness return as I considered the size of the new task before me. And yet at the same time I realized that the same God who had given me daily strength right up to that very day was still with me. I wasn't alone!

Alongside these immediate puzzle parts were other crucial factors like the support and blessing of the Brentwood congregation, my husband's encouragement, and the counsel of Charles and other significant people. After prayerfully considering all of this I eventually said yes to the Leadership Training Network opportunity.

The cycle of challenge, helplessness, growth, learning (so much learning!), and God's grace began again in my life. The same time factors that determined the launch of the vision at Brentwood governed the launch of LTN. From the beginning, I had the help of a great team. I enlisted a volunteer advisory board, which eventually became part of the teaching team. I have the continual joy of working alongside people who share my passion for equipping ministry.

One of LTN's core values is that only authentic practitioners will do training at our institutes and seminars. Our staff teaches what they practice. The ring of authenticity makes a difference. I've discovered this firsthand, as I've presented the equipping vision in groups that had strikingly different theological language and style from my own. When I tell the story of how Christ's body functions as an organism at Brentwood, I may not always use the same words they use, but I find I'm speaking a language they are longing to hear. I've learned that caring for, discovering, and growing God's people translates in any language.

Another powerful universal language is storytelling. Concepts and principles come alive in two ways: when you apply them to your own life and when you see them lived out in the lives of others. Somehow the living always has to come first—which is why I'm convinced that my LTN team must teach concepts and principles they've tested in the living laboratory of their own churches. The best illustrations come from our own experiences.

The principle of storytelling has governed the writing of this book. At the end of each chapter I've taken time to offer some of the principles we've learned along the way. There are, of course, many more to discover. Part of the reason I haven't tried to be exhaustive, or even exact, in following a pattern of development is that the flow of these principles will be unique to your setting. Remember, this never was about a program you can plug and play. This is about life in the body of Christ. I can't wait to hear the story of how you are living it!

THE JIM MARTIN STORY

IN MANY WAYS JIM MARTIN'S story captures so poignantly the results of spiritual transformation in a church. When people are identified, equipped, and released to do ministry according to biblical patterns, wonderful things happen. The philosophy, the details, and the lessons are part of the training and the journey. But the enduring results are wrapped up in the stories of real people into whom God has poured grace abounding.

Many of my stories about a certain person begin with other people. I might not have ever met that person or discovered his or her story if it hadn't been for someone else. I also mean I must begin Jim's story by talking about someone else. People grab our attention in the flow of life and make a difference, but they are there often because of other people. Parents, siblings, friends, and even enemies all contribute to a person's life before we meet him or her.

In church, we meet fellow travelers on life's sometimes difficult road. Each comes with a purpose. Sometimes they show up to make a difference. Sometimes they show up to hide and heal. Or perhaps they come to learn and grow. Often, the new people who come through our doors aren't sure why they came.

For all these reasons, I'm glad the first person newcomers typically meet in our church is Gordon. When they meet Gordon, they are in good hands. Gordon has a large dose of the gifts that make up what we call *hospitality.* He is observant, friendly, and tactful, and he possesses several other gifts that are too subtle to isolate but contribute to his unique character. He spots strangers and visitors, welcomes them, and engages them in conversation. He has a wonderful way of making people feel at home.

Many of the first contacts between our congregation and new people happen on the church patio (you may recall this from the story of Robert in chapter 7). Because of the southern California weather our church patio is an ideal gathering place before, between, and after services. It provides a safe transition zone between world and church. The patio is Gordon's favorite place to work his magic.

One Sunday Gordon caught sight of a young man slowly riding a bicycle back and forth past the church. Every few minutes he would ride by, casually observing the activities. He wore a pair of khaki Bermuda shorts, a T-shirt, and a bike helmet. He seemed to have a lot of time on his hands and no particular place to go.

After viewing a couple Sundays of this behavior, Gordon took action. He timed a stroll to the curb so that he was able to say a few words to the young man as he rode by. Gordon said hi to him on the first pass (it was a drive-by greeting). The young man returned the greeting in a deep and deliberate voice: "Hello." On the next pass Gordon invited him to stop for juice or a cup of coffee on the patio. The young man was reluctant, but Gordon matched him with gentle persistence. Eventually the young man pulled over and had some refreshments while Gordon engaged him in conversation. They exchanged names and began to connect.

It turned out that Jim Martin was in his thirties and out of work on extended disability. He had epilepsy. He lived alone. The helmet he wore while bike riding was a permanent part of his wardrobe—to protect his head during seizures. Although Jim's slow-motion speech pattern may have given the first impression that he was mentally handicapped, it was in reality a side effect of his medication. The medication, more than the epilepsy, also prevented him from being able to work. He was allowed to ride his bike, but not drive a car.

As the fellowship time came to a close that day, Gordon invited Jim to join him for the worship service. "No, I couldn't do that," answered Jim in his pondering baritone voice. "I'm just not dressed right." Undeterred, Gordon assured Jim that his outfit was just fine. He invited Jim to come the following Sunday, and he watched for him to show up. Jim did return, and Gordon began to connect him with other people, including me.

"Sue," Gordon said one Sunday as he approached me with Jim, "I'd like you to meet Jim Martin." As I greeted Jim, Gordon went on, "Jim, Sue will show you around here and help you find your way. That's what she does. You have any questions at all about what goes on around here, she's the first one to talk to." Jim was on his way to becoming a regular. We walked around the church for a while that day, and I made sure Jim knew where my office was located. "If you ever need any help, Jim," I said, "just come on in."

Gordon handed Jim off to me as part of an intentional way to assimilate new people. Their relationship continued, but Gordon had been the one to help Jim across the threshold into the rest of the church.

Since Gordon sang in the choir, he couldn't sit with Jim during the worship service. Within a week or two, Jim approached me with a question. His speech pattern was unforgettable. It reminded me of a dyed-in-the-wool southern California vocabulary expressed in a thoughtful, methodical cadence. "Can anyone sing in the choir?" "All you have to do is show up for practice on Thursday nights, Jim," I answered. That was all it took. Jim came to choir. He was warmly welcomed.

The next time a new-member class was offered Jim showed up. He intended to participate fully. He told his story and endeared himself to the rest of the class. For many of them it was an introduction to the unfamiliar world of an epileptic. Once we had talked it through, Jim's condition began to lose its intimidating power. We all got to know and appreciate the person wearing the helmet, and the helmet became an incidental feature rather than a separating or awkward item.

Jim's schedule allowed him to spend a lot of time around the church. He often hung out in my office. Our conversations revolved around various facets of my work. He was delightfully inquisitive.

"What are you doing there, Sue?" he asked one day, as I was gathering teaching materials.

"I'm getting ready for a leadership training session tonight, Jim," I answered.

"Boy, I've always wanted to be a leader," he said.

That comment got my attention! I asked, "What does that mean to you? What does it mean to be a leader, Jim?"

After a moment's reflection he answered, "Oh, you know. In charge of something. Helping people out. Just . . . being a leader. In charge of something."

I could hear the longing in his voice. "I think you would be a really good leader, Jim. Tell me, what are some of the things you like to do?"

"Well," he began, "there are a lot of things I can't do. 'Cause I can't drive a car, you know. But there are a lot of things I can do."

Now he really had my curiosity stirred up. "So, what are some of those things you do?"

As it turned out, Jim was a carpenter. He couldn't pursue his trade regularly because of his medication, but he made complicated wood puzzles in his workshop at home. He was quite a craftsman. And he had a number of other special abilities we were to discover later on.

Just before we headed out to Mexico to run one of our frequent work camps, Jim stopped by my office. "Sure wish I could go on that trip," he said.

"Is there a reason you can't?" I asked, thinking he would be a wonderful asset to the team.

"Oh, my health," he answered. "The doctor won't let me do that." His disappointment was obvious.

"Well," I suggested, "there are other ways to be involved even if you can't go yourself. We need all kinds of food to bring along. You could help out in the kitchen. . . ."

He thought the suggestion over for a moment and then said with a smile, "I make really good chocolate-chip cookies."

"Jim, do you have any idea how good chocolate-chip cookies would taste when we come back to our tents after working all day long at the work site?" I said.

"Okay, I'm going to bake some," he decided.

That first year Jim showed up on the day before the trip, carrying about a hundred dozen chocolate-chip cookies. The kids thought they had died and gone to heaven. Jim had provided not only a delicious treat, he had provided an *abundant* delicious treat. There were enough cookies to go around for everyone. Our snack times were like the feeding of the five thousand, when Jesus multiplied the loaves and fish, everyone had their fill, and there were twelve basketfuls left over!

Jim's cookies were a hit; they became a traditional part of the yearly Mexico work camps. If he knew a staff retreat was taking place, he would provide cookies. His special cookies became a signature in the life of our church. Events came to their most fitting conclusions with Jim's cookies.

Jim's carpentry skills also found a place of service. Because a large renovation project closed our sanctuary for a time, we transformed our gymnasium into the worship area. Jim helped make the temporary risers for the choir and prepare the area for this special use.

Meanwhile, his visits in my office continued to include conversations about leadership. He longed to find ways to serve what he saw as his family—the church. The following year I nominated Jim for a position

among the deacons. In our church culture, deacons carry out a shep-
herding, caregiving role within the congregation. The nominating committee contacted me with some skepticism. Actually, they thought I was
a little crazy. "Why do you think Jim Martin could be a deacon?" they
asked. I was glad they called. Some had not met him, others knew only
of his choir participation, and still others knew he had health challenges.
None of them knew him the way I had come to know him.

"I nominated Jim to be a deacon because he knows what it's like to
really care," I responded. "He's incredibly responsible. And he has a
desire to do this service." After a good deal of prayer and consideration,
the church called Jim to be a deacon. He was thrilled! In his amazing way
of seeing things, Jim summed up the depth of his response to this special invitation: "Now I'm really part of the family!"

I had the privilege of watching the process of taking on a leadership
role through Jim's eyes. We talked about everything. He couldn't wait for
the new-officer orientation. His enthusiasm for training made it exciting
to plan the session. Unfortunately, my mother had a serious health setback that caused us to postpone the orientation session that Charles and
I typically led together. The situation became an extended stressful time,
as my mother's health steadily worsened and her days with us rapidly
drew to a close. During the six weeks that my mother's life hung in the
balance, I was forced to postpone the new-officer training three times.
The first time I was able to call each leader and explain the postpone-
ment, but after that the situation became so hectic that I had the office
team take care of my apologies. As unavoidable as these cancellations
were, I remember feeling particularly sad to disappoint Jim. I tried to
make sure he understood the reasons behind the postponements, because
I didn't want him to feel in any way that his training wasn't important.

During the final week of my mother's life I was out of my office the
entire time. She died on the Sunday after Thanksgiving. The news of her
death was announced in church. The following Monday I arrived at my
office at 7:30 A.M., grieving and facing the daunting task of organizing the
chaos of all that had accumulated over the previous month. I felt that
immersing myself in my work would genuinely help me. I needed the
structure, the fellowship, and the life that surrounded me at the church.

When I turned on the lights in my office, it took just one glance, and
I was overwhelmed by the piles of mail and messages that threatened to
cascade off my desk. Well, I had to start somewhere. So I made my way
around my desk and pulled out the chair to sit down. There, resting on
my chair, was a container of warm chocolate-chip cookies. Jim had been
there ahead of me. He knew what I would very likely do in this situation
and "ran ahead" to find a way to help me. I sat in the chair with the cook-

ies on my lap, mail and chaos momentarily forgotten, knowing I was cared for deeply by others in God's family.

Like most real servants, Jim was already ministering to others before we gave him a title. The training we gave him only supplemented what God had already given him. We had the privilege of benefiting from Jim's wonderful gifts.

He took over the food pantry as a personal responsibility. He brought a real sense of purpose and order to our outreach to the homeless in our community. He kept the pantry stocked as never before. Along the way Jim also took over as our coordinator of emergency transportation. Now, remember, he couldn't drive. Some might have seen this as an obvious reason not to consider him for such a role; we concluded that there were a couple of strong reasons why he *should* be in the role: first, there was no danger that he would think he could do this job on his own (after all, he couldn't drive!), and second, he understood from personal experience the importance of personal transportation and the frustrations that come with depending on others for rides. He led in a beautiful way by providing opportunities for others to serve.

Jim did a stellar job as a deacon. He loved the role. He turned his limitations into limitless service.

TRIP TO YOSEMITE

DURING THIS TIME THE lay ministries team of our church was continually expanding. My increasing duties led to a move to a larger office with more space but fewer storage and organizing features. I was particularly short on bookshelf space. Piles of binders, folders, and books threatened to take over the office. Jim and I were visiting one day during one of his stop-bys, and he pointed out the obvious. "Place is sure a mess," he observed in his unmistakable baritone cadence. He didn't mince words. "You sure need some shelves," he added.

"You bet I do," I responded. "I'd give just about anything to get this stuff organized."

"I could probably build those for you," he offered.

Hope rose within me. "Really? Do you have the time?" I asked.

"Yup," he said. "You get the wood, and I'll build them. You got a tape?"

I rushed to get him a tape measure, and he proceeded to take all kinds of dimension measurements of my office. He gave me a list of wood to get. "You get me this wood, and I'll build the shelves. But I can't do it until Monday."

I could hardly believe my ears. I was used to church-project schedules, which always seem to mean months of waiting for things to get done.

Jim had a plan already. "I'll be back on Monday. You have that wood here." Then he added, "Till then I'm going on a trip."

"Where are you going?" I asked.

"I'm going to Yosemite. I've always wanted to see that big rock!" he explained.

I thought I knew what he was saying. "You mean Half Dome?"

He nodded, "Half Dome. I'm going to go see Half Dome."

I was thrilled at the news and genuinely happy for Jim. "You have a great time, and we'll see you back here on Monday," I said.

It was to be my last conversation with Jim this side of eternity. I got a call during the weekend. Jim had died in Yosemite. He suffered a grand mal seizure, probably triggered by the high altitude, from which he did not recover.

Jim's unexpected death devastated our church. He had become such an integral part of our life together. It was difficult for the pastors to make the announcement during the worship service. The congregation's immediate emotional response was an outpouring of grief. The universal sense of loss gave testimony to Jim's impact. We had all been touched in one way or another by the life of this amazing man. He was a servant and leader. He was a deacon—through and through.

I will never forget the memorial service we held for Jim. Although he had no shortage of friends, he had no family in the area. His mother, who lived out of town, came to the service. The sanctuary was packed to overflowing. Story after story of Jim's compassion and practical bent kept us in tears and smiles throughout the memorial celebration of his life.

One gentleman in our church named Ron recounted a delightful exchange he had had with Jim. One day while driving to work Ron had spotted a parked ambulance. He also saw, much to his concern, what appeared to be Jim's bicycle lying on the street and a man being attended by the medical personnel. He stopped and discovered that the victim was, in fact, Jim, who had suffered a seizure and was resting on the ambulance gurney. Relieved after verifying that Jim wasn't hurt, Ron had leaned over him and said the first thing that came to mind: "Jim, you ran into a truck." Jim thought for a moment and then answered, "Ronny, did I hurt it?"

The rich storytelling allowed us to experience and express our grief in good ways. We had all lost a gentle friend. But it turned out that Jim wasn't finished serving us. Several months later, the church administrator came into a staff meeting with tears streaming down her cheeks. In her hand she held a check from an insurance company. Jim had taken out a policy on his life and made his family—the church—the beneficiaries.

Jim had often commented that we lacked a place in our facilities for people to be quiet and reflective. Charles had possessed that same vision.

Both envisioned a prayer garden in a space behind our fellowship hall. Jim's money, along with another gift of money, was set aside for the creation of the Jim Martin Memorial Garden. (And, as you will read in the postscript, Jim Martin's gift has come to serve in yet another significant way in our life as a church.)

WHAT'S YOUR DREAM?

AS YOU COME TO the end of this book, are you like one of the people who would come up during a break and say, "Great stories, but I don't think it can happen in my church"?

Whatever your present role in the church is, let me acknowledge your feelings of helplessness. I've been there. Let me also tell you the one thing you must remember. It has kept me going when every plan seems to be going amiss. It has brought me out of hurts, anger, disappointments, impatience, and yes, helplessness.

In those times (and there have been many of them, actually) when I have thought, and even murmured out loud, "I don't think it can happen in my church," I can almost hear Jesus' voice whispering to catch my attention: "If that's all it is, then it really won't happen. Remember, it isn't just your church—it's MY CHURCH!"

> ... on this rock I will build my church, and the gates of Hades will not overcome it.
>
> Matthew 16:18

QUESTIONS FOR REFLECTION AND DISCUSSION

1. If you are in the process of calling someone to take on the role of equipping leader, what are the qualities and gifts you are seeking above and beyond the credentials and the qualifications?

2. Take some time to look at Jim's story yet again. Identify and list some of the systems that allowed Jim to flourish in ministry.

3. Who are your "stories"? Invite them to share their stories in the context of ministry and worship.

4. What are your roadblocks to becoming an equipping church? Consider entering a season of prayer, and reflect on how you can allow God to accompany you on the journey. Offer up your roadblocks, then listen for God's plan in your church.

Postscript

THE EQUIPPING CHURCH won't sit still for a picture because there's just too much going on. Thus, even the word pictures of the principles and the people and the events that make up the life of an equipping church are never complete. After all, the body of Christ is a living organism, made up of living parts that are constantly changing. They learn, grow, age, and some of them die. New brothers and sisters become part of the body and take their place. Christ continues to pour out his gifts on his church in and through his people.

In the year or so that it has taken to bring this book to completion, a lot has happened. That is life. I have thought much about how to capture the "life goes on" aspects of this vast story without having the language become too complicated or the explanations too long.

When I began the first chapter of this book, my husband and I were deeply involved in Charles's struggle against cancer. There were long vigils at the hospital and at his bedside at home. Moments of hope mixed with hours of pain and despair. Those remain very precious days and nights in our lives.

On the occasion of his last birthday here on earth I was able to present to Charles several of the early chapters of this book. He smiled. As has been true for me, I don't think he could separate the joy over what God had already done and is doing among us at Brentwood from the joy over seeing what God was doing in other places as the vision spread.

It was during the time I was writing the middle chapters that Charles lost the struggle. He was only fifty-six years old. Our friend had fought the good fight and had kept the faith to the end. Those of us who knew him lost a leader, mentor, cheerleader, and friend. He modeled so many Christlike character traits that he left an indelible impression on the medical personnel who attended him, many people from outside the church, and of course the congregation that he loved so much. This book has become as much as anything a tribute to the biblical vision that Charles brought to Brentwood and the lives that continue to be transformed as a result.

In chapter 11 I told the story of Jim Martin, who in so many ways contributed to and benefited from the body of Christ at Brentwood. At his death he left a lasting legacy in the form of a memorial garden, a refuge Charles deeply appreciated. The space provided an intimate setting for worship and a place for serious conversation, prayer, and reflection. A place to meet God.

This place has also come to remind all of us that buildings may surround and shelter the church, but they are not the church. This quiet space helps us remember that *we* are the church. Fittingly, Charles's family will honor his legacy in a final private service to take place in the Jim Martin Memorial Garden. What better way to honor his commitment to and his love of Christ's church. In a time-honored tradition, the body of Jesus Christ continues to build on the foundation of the saints who have gone before.

Meanwhile I can't help but think that Charles is enjoying himself thoroughly, dancing and cheering with that "great cloud of witnesses" (Hebrews 12:1), as he, along with the Lord, watches the amazing living miracle called the church.

In memory of Charles Edward Shields
1944–2000
Christ "gave . . . some to be pastors"

The Equipping Church

LEADERSHIP
training
NETWORK

Providing personal, relational, Christ-centered growth through ministry in the church, community, world, and the whole of life

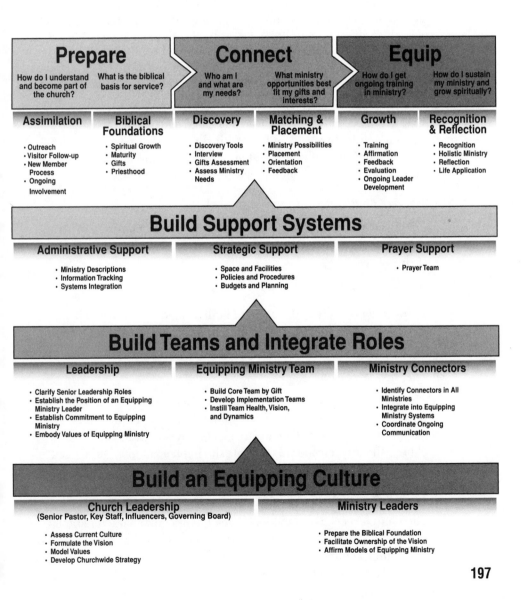

Prepare		**Connect**		**Equip**	
How do I understand and become part of the church?	What is the biblical basis for service?	Who am I and what are my needs?	What ministry opportunities best fit my gifts and interests?	How do I get ongoing training in ministry?	How do I sustain my ministry and grow spiritually?
Assimilation	**Biblical Foundations**	**Discovery**	**Matching & Placement**	**Growth**	**Recognition & Reflection**
• Outreach • Visitor Follow-up • New Member Process • Ongoing Involvement	• Spiritual Growth • Maturity • Gifts • Priesthood	• Discovery Tools • Interview • Gifts Assessment • Assess Ministry Needs	• Ministry Possibilities • Placement • Orientation • Feedback	• Training • Affirmation • Feedback • Evaluation • Ongoing Leader Development	• Recognition • Holistic Ministry • Reflection • Life Application

Build Support Systems

Administrative Support	**Strategic Support**	**Prayer Support**
• Ministry Descriptions • Information Tracking • Systems Integration	• Space and Facilities • Policies and Procedures • Budgets and Planning	• Prayer Team

Build Teams and Integrate Roles

Leadership	**Equipping Ministry Team**	**Ministry Connectors**
• Clarify Senior Leadership Roles • Establish the Position of an Equipping Ministry Leader • Establish Commitment to Equipping Ministry • Embody Values of Equipping Ministry	• Build Core Team by Gift • Develop Implementation Teams • Instill Team Health, Vision, and Dynamics	• Identify Connectors in All Ministries • Integrate into Equipping Ministry Systems • Coordinate Ongoing Communication

Build an Equipping Culture

Church Leadership (Senior Pastor, Key Staff, Influencers, Governing Board)	**Ministry Leaders**
• Assess Current Culture • Formulate the Vision • Model Values • Develop Churchwide Strategy	• Prepare the Biblical Foundation • Facilitate Ownership of the Vision • Affirm Models of Equipping Ministry

Core Values of an Equipping Church

❖ *Prayer*

The equipping church recognizes the inherent value of prayer to discern God's vision, leadership, and plan toward an equipping ministry model. Equipping church leaders rely on prayer to see God in all aspects of their ministry.

❖ *The Priesthood of All Believers and the Vision of the Church as Contained in Ephesians 4*

Every member in the body of Christ is gifted and called into ministry. The church embraces people holistically in the discovery of gifts, needs, and God's calling. The church seeks to equip people for ministry in the family, the church, the community, and the world.

❖ *Servant Leadership*

Leaders demonstrate humility, authenticity, accountability, and genuine care of people, and they equip others to use their gifts in the body of Christ.

❖ *Team Ministry*

Healthy community and teams are built around the individuality of gifts, team accountability, and willingness of people to work for the good of the greater body.

❖ *Intentionality*

The church embraces equipping ministry as a value and models it through the intentional implementation of systems to prepare, connect, and equip people for ministry inside and outside the walls of the church. It calls a leader to facilitate the implementation throughout the body of Christ.

❖ *Proactive Response to Change*

The church recognizes and embraces the organic characteristic of change and responds creatively and proactively to shifts in culture. The church continually changes her methods, but maintains the message of Christ regarding his church.

Developing an Equipping Church

The charts on the following pages show all the elements essential for developing a church oriented toward equipping ministry. The chart "How to Change the Culture" begins with assessing what is needed to prepare the way for any constructive change. The second chart "How to Build the System" pictures the larger systemic principles that must be met in order to honor the organic life of the body of Christ.

Depending on the existing components in any particular church, the starting points may not be identical, but the eventual flow will follow this course. In the chart you will see a correlation between the flow we have analyzed from our work with many congregations and how our Brentwood story has followed this basic process of transformation.

The bottom half of each chart represents the foundational work that falls under the responsibility of the church leadership and the equipping ministry team. The top elements of each chart are the experiences, questions, and participation of the individual members in the life of the church. The degree to which these are achieved will measure how much each member will be able to grow toward full connectedness and maturity. The process is never as linear as the chart makes it seem to be, but the chart helps to visualize the connections and the way the process tends to work.

You will note that many of the experiences and adventures you read about in the book are reflected in these charts. The two charts overlap in content in places and offer a number of checkpoints with which you can chart your progress. The questions that accompany each of the significant steps require thoughtful attention. If you cannot answer them yourself, invite others to help you discover the answers. As always, the process is intended to be widely inclusive, even though it will, in practice, start with a smaller group that makes up the original team.

How to Change the Culture

(1) ASSESS

What is the current culture of our church?

How is our culture communicated?

How does our existing program emphasis reflect our culture?

What and where is our readiness for change?

(2) ENVISION

Where do we want to go?

Who do we want to be?

Who needs to be involved in formulating the vision?

Who needs to own the vision for it to be realized?

Who has the responsibility and necessary gifts to
communicate and expand the vision?

(3) EMBODY VALUES

How do I, our team, and the church leadership incarnate target values?

Where do we need to change/grow?

How do we facilitate change in our leadership team?

(4) STRATEGIZE

How do we reach our desired future state?

How do we move churchwide culture toward the vision?

LEADERSHIP

DEVELOPMENT

(5) PREPARE THE FOUNDATION

How do we lay the biblical framework and foundation for the vision with the church?

(6) CAST THE VISION

How do we share the vision with the church body so that each person can see his or her place in it?

(7) AFFIRM MODELS

What good examples/models are there within the church to affirm?

How to Build the System

Vision, Strategy, and Team

What and why are we building?
What is the vision for gift-based team ministry?

Who am I as leader?
What do I bring to the ministry?
What do I need to take care of myself?

Where are we now?
In our church what current systems are in place for. . .
- Assimilation and Biblical Foundations?
- Discovery, Matching, and Placement?
- Training, Affirmation, Feedback, and Evaluation?
- Leader Development, Recognition, and Reflection?

Who are the builders?
How do we select and build the equipping ministry leadership team?

Where do we go from here?
Vision casting
Strategic planning

How do we work together?
Team dynamics

INTEGRATE
How do we integrate equipping ministry into existing church systems?

SUPPORT

CONNECT
How do we connect people, church, and community?

- Discovery
  - The interview as ministry

- Matching and Placement:
  - Church connections
  - Community connections

PREPARE
How do we reach out to people and bring them into the church?

- Assimilation
- Biblical foundations

SYSTEMS

EQUIP
How do we equip people in ministry?

- Training
- Affirmation
- Feedback
- Evaluation
- Leader Development
- Recognition
- Reflection

LEADERSHIP
training
NETWORK

The mission of Leadership Training Network is to influence and resource innovative church leaders to equip people for biblical, gift-based team ministry. Since 1995 Leadership Training Network (LTN) has provided church leaders with resources designed to help transition their congregations into equipping churches.

Events: LTN Institutes

Institutes offer hands-on training for church leaders in all stages of equipping church development, led by authentic practitioners who build peer networks of other equipping ministry leaders.

Products

Books

The Equipping Church: Serving Together to Transform Lives
by Sue Mallory

Sue Mallory's story of becoming the director of equipping ministries in a California church serves as a framework to explain what an equipping church is, how an equipping church functions, why this is a biblical model, and what is involved in making this transition.

The Equipping Church Guidebook
by Sue Mallory and Brad Smith

This revised version of *The Starter Kit for Mobilizing Ministry* includes new learnings and models developed since the initial publication in 1995. Based on research done with hundreds of churches across North America, this resource is useful for paid and unpaid staff members, lay leaders, and denominational leaders.

Training Modules

Tools designed to help leaders train others. Each module includes a leader's guide, participant handouts, overhead transparency masters, and a CD containing customizable versions of the handouts and PowerPoint slides.

Who Am I As a Leader?   *Building Support Systems for Equipping Ministry*

Writing Ministry Descriptions   *Inviting People into Ministry*

Interviewing Skills

Assessment Tools

Tools designed to help you assess all aspects of your church systems and culture.

Administrative Systems Assessment Tool   *Task Management: Systems*

The Equipping Church Chart   *Task Management: Culture*

Audio, Video, Web, and E-mail Products

Strategies for Equipping Ministry—kit includes participant manual and six audiotapes

NCNC Vision Video—excellent vision-casting tool for church boards and key leaders

e-COR—over one hundred best resources categorized in a searchable database on the LTN Web site at www.ltn.org

e.quipper—a free monthly on-line publication

Leadership Network

Leadership Training Network is a partner with Leadership Network. Founded in 1984, its mission is to accelerate the emergence of effective churches by identifying, connecting, and resourcing innovative church leaders.

www.leadnet.org.

To order or subscribe contact:

Leadership Training Network
2501 Cedar Springs, Suite 200
Dallas, TX 75201
Phone: 877-LTN-LEAD (586-5323)
Fax: 214-969-9392
Web: www.LTN.org

The Equipping Church Guidebook
Your Comprehensive Resource
Sue Mallory and Brad Smith

This guidebook starts with the biblical mandate to leaders from Ephesians 4:11–15, emerging not out of a theory of how this mandate should be achieved, but out of a journalistic effort to describe the best models of hundreds of churches who are doing healthy equipping ministry. It translates what was found in these healthy and innovative models into transferable principles, examples, questions, and exercises to help other church leaders build an equipping ministry tailored to meet the needs and calling of their own church.

This is a hands-on ministry resource guide to help churches develop leaders and systems for lay mobilization. The approach is open-ended so that a variety of types and sizes of churches can use it. Charts and worksheets are included. The material has been tested through several years of use in churches that received the privately distributed notebook format, titled *The Starter Kit for Mobilizing Ministry*. Now updated and extensively revised, this volume serves as a practical companion to *The Equipping Church*, which provides the philosophy and challenging vision for lay mobilization.

Part One: Building an Equipping Ministry Vision and Culture
Part Two: Building an Equipping Ministry System

Softcover   ISBN: 0-310-23957-5

ZONDERVAN™

GRAND RAPIDS, MICHIGAN 49530

www.zondervan.com

LEADERSHIP ✳ NETWORK

We want to hear from you. Please send your comments about this book to us in care of the address below. Thank you.

ZONDERVAN™

GRAND RAPIDS, MICHIGAN 49530
www.zondervan.com